I0469036

Become Super-Productive:

Get more out of life!

David Suescun

DISCLAIMERS:

Although the author have made every effort to ensure that the information in this book was correct at publish time, the author do not assume and hereby disclaim any liability to any party for any loss, damage, or disruption caused by errors or omissions, whether such errors or omissions result from negligence, accident, or any other cause.

This book is not intended as a substitute for the medical advice of physicians. The reader should regularly consult a physician in matters relating to his/her health and particularly with respect to any symptoms that may require diagnosis or medical attention.

To all my loved ones, from all species.

Learning goals

At the end of this book, readers will be able to:

- Create healthy habits.
- Harvest their Body, Mental, Emotional and Spiritual Energy.
- Use their resources (time and money) more effectively.
- Work & Communicate better with others.
- Use technology (apps, software and web services) to automate tasks and maximize their productivity.
- Set up efficient Content/Knowledge systems.

Who should read this book?

- Anyone who is interested in becoming more productive at school, at work, and in their personal life.
- Anyone who wants to create a more engaging lifestyle.
- Anyone who enjoys learning new things.
- Anyone who will start a new role and wants to prepare for it.
- Anyone who finds the Author's blog interesting (http://blog.deft.xyz/.)
- This book isn't intended for those who are not willing to work hard towards their goals. This book doesn't contain a magic fix-all formula.

TABLE OF CONTENTS

Acknowledgments

I would like to thank my brother Oscar Suescun and my sister Nathalia Suescun for their endless revisions, comments, and suggestions. This book wouldn't have been possible without their contributions, especially my brother's that made the book a lot more enjoyable.

I would also like to thank my friends, who helped me proof-read the manuscript and provided their insight and comments.

Last but not least, I would like to thank my parents (Hermes Suescun & Lucy Ramirez) for everything they've done for me.

Chapter 1: Introduction

Hi! Welcome to "Become Super-Productive: Get More Out of Life"!

This book is designed to help anyone who wants to increase their productivity at school, at work, or even at home. And is not about doing things fast for the sake of speed, but for the sake of improving your life, while giving your best to your activities.

There are no knowledge pre-requisites to get the most out of this book, so if this is your first approach to increasing productivity, you've definitively come to right place. Even if you've already explored some techniques from other resources, there's something here for you too. We'll start by covering some key concepts and principles that will help you maximize the impact of your efforts. They will help you set yourself up for success. After that, we will go through the power of habits and how to build or modify them. You'll also learn some cool actionable, and specific techniques for:

- Time Management
- Energy Management
- Communications Management
- Information Management

So after each section, you'll be able to do more, with less.

Now, if you're wondering what qualifies me to write this book, let me tell you a little bit about myself.

My name is David Suescun; I was born and raised in Colombia. I studied Mechatronics Engineering and started working in the Energy Industry in Sudan (Africa) right after graduation. I've since traveled to 25 countries on 4 continents, for both work and pleasure. I speak Spanish, English, French and Portuguese.

The nature of my work kept me away from home for very long periods of time, so in 2014 I decided to quit my job and spend some time with my family and regain control of some things I didn't like in my life. That's when I learned French, learned how to speed read, lost 10 pounds, quit smoking, got rid of 60% of my stuff, organized my finances and learned how to develop mobile apps. All of this in 4 months. I then worked in Gabon as a Service Delivery Manager for West Africa for over a year. It was my first big time management assignment, so for the first three months I was working from Sunday to Sunday trying to stay on top of everything and prove my worth. I had the same experience during short assignments in sales and operations' management before, so I decided to use my accelerated learning skills to become super productive and reclaim my life! After that I worked remotely for one month, so successfully that some of my peers didn't realize that I was working from Colombia, and with a six hours' time difference! Not only that, for the remaining of the year I took over the field operations management role -on top of mine-, and managed a daily routine that allowed me to leave every day at 5 pm, never work on weekends and complete over 25 university-level online courses. Plus I prepared all my meals and exercised routinely.

The techniques you'll learn here are time tested.

I've done my best to keep the sections short, and spare you the details of the research that backs what you're about to read. Nonetheless, I'll provide plenty of resources that you can explore outside this book to feed your curiosity.

My knowledge comes from actual experience and research. I've read tons of books, and done tons of courses on productivity, and I know first-hand how sometimes the "best-sellers" produced by "self-employed" authors do not fit the actual needs of everyday workers. That's why I've put a lot of effort in curating the content of this book to ensure that both entrepreneurs and workers alike get the most actionable methods to productivity.

Thank you for being here, and welcome! I hope you enjoy the book as much as I enjoyed writing it!

PS: You can join our Facebook Community Page to share with others that are also embarking into becoming super productive:
http://deft.xyz/1pi7DlX

Chapter 2: Key Concepts & Principles

How This Chapter Came To Be

Before digging in with the key concepts and principles for being super-productive, let me share with you my experience over my first two months after joining the workforce.

I was hired by Schlumberger, the biggest Oil & Gas Service Company in the world, to work in Sudan, Africa. For me, it was a great deal. To my knowledge, I was the first engineer hired from my university, and this is an Elite company known for challenging training programs and excellent work results, so the stakes were high. Even before signing the contract, the company flew me to the other side of the world: Kuala Lumpur, Malaysia and accommodated me and another 60 new hires from all over the world to give us our first week of training. After making things official, I traveled to Sudan for a two months hands-on experience.

During this time I was working every day from 7 am to 7 pm, and studying the training material until 3 am. It was exhausting.

After the two months, my energy levels were very low. I never took any time to rest because the base was remote -in the middle of the jungle- and the working schedule was from Sunday to Sunday, so nowhere to go and no days off. My knowledge retention was very low as well. By overworking myself I became very ineffective. I was dedicating a lot of time to learn small details that didn't really have any impact or place in "the big picture."

After barely passing the test to be admitted into the three-month training school, I had the opportunity to spend one week in Cairo, Egypt, while getting my visa to go to the training center in Canada. During this week, I decided to study again, but, this time, using my university practices: study with breaks and make time to relax and enjoy the experience, contrary to stress and study non-stop like I had tried before. I chose to focus on the most important things only. The strategy paid off, I had to retake the exam on arrival to the training center, and I scored 10 points higher than my initial score. We'll go through the techniques I used later in this chapter.

Some of the concepts and principles you'll find in this chapter might seem counterintuitive depending on your own experience and beliefs, so it is understandable and expected that you will question some of the ideas expressed here. The most important thing to keep in mind is that you should question these concepts with an open mind and an honest desire to make the most for your own wellbeing and success.

Let's start from the beginning. The first key concept we should talk about if we want to learn how to be more productive is the motivation to do so. What makes you want to keep learning even after you've graduated from school? What drives adults to learn?

What Drives Adults to Learn?

"I cannot teach anybody anything; I can only make them think."
- Socrates

"Anyone who stops learning is old, whether at twenty or eighty.
Anyone who keeps learning stays young."
- Henry Ford

There's a general misunderstanding that adults can't learn as well, or as fast, as younger people. This misconception probably comes from the fact that adults have different motivations for learning, and the methods that work for children and teenagers are probably not very effective for adults.

The concept of adult learning, also known as "andragogy", was pioneered by Malcolm Knowles between the 50's and the 70's. He identified six adult learning principles, which may apply a little to children, but are much truer in adults. These principles state that adults:

1. **Are internally motivated and self-directed**
2. **Bring life experiences, and knowledge, to their learning experiences**
3. **Are goal oriented**
4. **Are relevancy oriented**
5. **Are practical**
6. **Like to be respected**

You might be asking yourself: how do I benefit from knowing these principles? And that's an excellent question! By understanding them, and applying them, you'll be able to stay engaged with the book. You will also understand that the contents aim towards a goal, and nothing is random here.

Let's go through the principles one by one:

1. Adults are internally motivated and self-directed:

Being internally motivated and self-directed means that **adults do things that they think are important for them**, not what others think is important. How can you use this in your favor? Whenever deciding to acquire a new piece of knowledge, in any form, try drawing a mental picture of how you might use that knowledge.

This is much easier said than done. Many of us are so self-sufficient that we trick ourselves into believing we know "all" there is to know about something, or at least enough to dismiss new information before we have even taken a look at it. In those cases, I find it very useful to re-frame that challenge to overconfidence as a great opportunity to find more about other perspectives on the subject, and that way I can make my own ideas stronger. This means questioning those perspectives and using my ideas, or knowledge, to defeat them, which may, or may not, result in re-evaluating my beliefs, or organizing them better.

2. Adults bring life experiences and knowledge to their learning experiences:

As we grow older, we also grow wiser and more experienced. We use this knowledge and experience to relate to the things we are about to learn.

You can use this principle by trying to fit the new knowledge into your experiences: what would you have done differently? How could you have benefited from that knowledge back when you had those experiences? This will also align with the first principle as this will help you get internally motivated to learn.

3. Adults are goal oriented:

When we are growing up, our learning topics tend to be grouped, so we learn in a subject-oriented manner. As we start entering adulthood, we become more problem-oriented, so we want to learn things that will help us solve specific problems.

That's probably one of the reasons you're here: you've identified a problem or opportunity for improvement, and you actively want to gain knowledge on how to tackle it.

4. Adults are relevancy oriented:

Adults are most interested in learning matters that are immediately relevant to their life.

But don't be too quick to discard things that might appear irrelevant to your current situation, or problems. Remember what we said before, you can visualize and project yourself facing new problems in the future, and thus get the internal motivation to learn something new in the present, so you can solve problems when they come.

5. Adults are practical:

When we're about to learn something, we want to be pragmatic: we need to know in advance what's in it for us. If this question is not quickly answered, you can always look it up, or even ask. It depends on how you like to learn.

If you are thinking about learning something from a non-fiction book, for example, try looking at the conclusions, you might even decide to completely avoid the book. If it's a skill-based course, ask to see some of the previous students' achievements. The review section is usually helpful as well.

6. Adult learners like to be respected:

As adults, we value our self-concept, and it's very easy to dismiss new information if we believe our knowledge and experience are not being respected by whoever is providing the new information.

You can benefit from this principle by internalizing this: no one benefits more than you from learning something new. So if someone struggles communicating something respectfully, or gracefully, try to focus on the message and filter out the form it's coming in.

And that's all I have to say about that, as Forrest Gump would say. Now that you know the basics of keeping you motivated while learning, we'll go through the concept of setting goals.

Preparation: Setting Goals

> *"By failing to prepare you are preparing to fail."*
> - Benjamin Franklin

The first step towards productivity is learning how to set goals. More often than not we set our expectations too high, and we end up being discouraged even before we start working to fulfill them. Sometimes we are too vague in the way we describe our goals, leaving us idle, with no clear direction on what to do next.

When it comes to how to choose your goals don't just focus on the day-to-day stuff. Make sure that you set goals in the long run too. Everything else should become a building stepping stone towards that. And one way of setting powerful goals in both those cases can be achieved using the main idea in the book "The ONE Thing", by Gary Keller and Jay Papasan. They argue that there's ONE thing that you can do, that if done will make all the other things easier, or unnecessary.

So once you have a good idea of the goals you want to set for yourself, or your subordinates, we can use this neat technique for setting objectives. Enter the S.M.A.R.T objectives. There are several variations of this acronym, and the one I like the most is this one:
S: Specific
M: Measurable
A: Achievable
R: Relevant
T: Time-bounded

Specific:
When you're setting up your goals, be as specific as you can. One way of putting it, is that your goal should answer the 5 'W' questions: What, why, who, where, which.

Measurable:
Try to make the definition of success something you can measure, or quantify. This will help you identify when you have reached the goal.

Achievable:
Make sure you are aiming for something you can achieve. This doesn't mean "aim low", it just means that you should respect your own limits and boundaries.

Relevant:
There's no point in becoming very effective in doing something that won't have an impact on the big picture. Your goals should be set in the right direction so that they're relevant.

Time-Bounded:
Time has two functions in this system, depending on the length required to complete the goal. But in general, you should define time-bounded checkpoints to review your progress in completing the goal, and you should define the deadline for when you expect or need to complete the goal. You need to answer the "when" question.

Ok, let's put the S.M.A.R.T pieces together in an example, let's have a look at a typical New Year's resolution list:

For 2016, I want to:
-    Lose weight
-    drink more water

Now, these goals are too vague; there's nothing there that will keep you going because it's an endless road! Lose weight until you disappear? Drink more water by having an extra half a glass of water daily?

If we apply the S.M.A.R.T technique we could come up with something like:

-   Lose 10 lb of fat by the end of the year. 7 lb of total weight by mid-year (June 30).
-   Drink 1 gallon of water per day: 1 liter (4 glasses) before 9 am, 1 liter before 12 am, 1 liter between 2 pm and 4 pm and finally 1 liter between 4 pm and 7 pm.

Now that we know how to set S.M.A.R.T goals, we'll move to the next logical step, getting ready for execution.

Preparation: Mise en Place

"If I had eight hours to chop down a tree, I'd spend six sharpening my axe."
- Abraham Lincoln

Mise en place is a French expression commonly used in the culinary world. It means: put in place. If you've ever seen a cooking program, you might have noticed how all the ingredients are placed in the cooking table before the chef starts cooking. This preparation helps the chef to be more efficient. Once you've set up your goals, then you want to work in preparing the things that you'll need to complete them.

If we take the New Years' resolution example, I now know what I need to prepare:

- I need to get myself measured at the gym, or with a physician. This way I'll know my current fat percentage, which multiplied by my weight will give my weight coming from fat, which I've planned to reduce by 10 lb.
- I need to find a digital scale that measures body fat percentage to keep an eye on it, and follow my progress.
- I need to find a way to measure my water intake; an easy thing would be to buy a 1-liter water bottle so I can keep track easily.
- I need to set alarms throughout the day to make sure I drink the whole bottle before each checkpoint.

So, not only do I have some ideas on how to start working on my goals, but I can also see myself achieving them if I break down the process into separate milestones, and by setting up the tools required for the job. The *Mise en Place* will be used in several parts of this book, even if we don't call it by that name.

Looking back to my own case, setting learning goals and doing a proper "mise en place", by choosing the critical material to study, was how I set myself in the right direction to correct my path.

And so, once we've established where we need to get, and we are prepared for it, at least physically, we also need some mental preparation. It's no use to be ready for a picnic with all your tools and food ready if you suddenly feel like you don't want to go out for a picnic after all. So, we need to examine the state of mind we need to get into; that's what we'll review in our next section.

Mindful vs. Stressed?

*"Life is a preparation for the future, and the best preparation for the
future is to live as if there were none."*
- Albert Einstein

"YOLO."
- Drake

"The best way to destroy an enemy is to make him a friend."
- Abraham Lincoln

The quote from Albert Einstein is there to highlight the importance of living the now, which is also the mantra behind mindfulness; a mental state of awareness. A quiet mind. Living fully the here and the now. This allows us to increase our happiness and creativity.

Abraham Lincoln's quote makes a good point on how to defeat an enemy by getting closer to it. In our case, stress has been portrayed as an evil force over the last decades. But in truth, it's the stressed state that has kept us alive for thousands of years. So we can take advantage of that seemingly negative element by befriending it. So, it's not mindful vs. stressed; it's mindfulness via stress. The perfect state of mind is a balance of both states. These can be re-phrased as relaxation and focus. Being focused is great, but focus is self-limiting; only by alternating focused and relaxed states can we fully unleash our potential for learning and creativity, and interconnect a wider spectrum of neural networks.

For me, during my two months training, the stressed state had terrible results, and I wasn't getting anywhere near where I needed to be. Only when I recognized the importance of allowing my mind and body to have moments to relax in a hazy glow, interspaced with laser focus moments, was I able to succeed in learning the material properly.

Some of the time management principles and techniques that we'll review are fueled by this concept. The next section, for example, will emphasize on the importance of recognizing the most impactful thing(s) to focus on.

Make sure to check out the Bibliography & Additional References(at the end of the book) on learning how to learn from Barbara Oakley, she explains how focused & relaxed states are useful in learning.

The 80/20 Pareto Principle

"People who create 20% of the results will begin believing they deserve 80% of the rewards."
- Pat Riley

The Pareto principle states that 80% of the outputs come from 20% of the inputs. This principle is something you are probably familiar with. It has been around for almost 100 years, and another way of stating it is to say that 20% of the work yields 80% of the results. It comes from Vilfredo Pareto, an Italian economist who noticed that 80% of Italy's wealth was in the hands of 20% of the population.

In a few different contexts, it might be expressed as:

- 80% of a company's profits come from 20% of its customers.
- 80% of a company's complaints come from 20% of its customers.
- 80% of a company's sales come from 20% of its products.
- 80% of a company's sales are made by 20% of its sales staff.

I learned about the Pareto Distribution in college but wasn't too interested in it until I read the 4-Hour Workweek by Tim Ferriss and saw it from a new perspective. Since I'm a learning enthusiast, I've tried this principle in different areas and found that this overall distribution holds true. For example:

In language learning:
- If you want to go at it in an analytical manner, you can decide to learn the most common words. To achieve this, you can search for the Word

frequencies for the most frequent 10,000 words. I did this for English, Spanish, and French, and as it turns out, there's 1,000 to 2,000 words that account for 80% of the frequency usage.

- I also applied this concept by taking 30% of a full French Course, and I managed to communicate effectively with French-speaking natives during my year in West Africa. I wouldn't go as far as to say that 30% of the course gave me 70% of fluency, but damn close to it.

In Quality Assurance:
- Over my last assignment, I was managing maintenance events, and to do so, we were constantly applying Root Cause Analysis (RCA) to the failures we had. It didn't come as a surprise that 80% of the failures were coming from 20% of the Root Causes.

What's really important here, is not the mathematical accuracy of the principle, but the concept of being able to achieve the highest impact with the minimum effort. And once you've internalized this, you can choose your tasks by analyzing the impact, and prioritize them from highest to lower.

That's exactly how I chose which material to study during my week in Cairo: I had to pick the documents that had the big picture concepts, had enough lingo for me to learn the ways of my industry, but not so complicated as to get lost in formulas I would never use. This selection meant browsing through 15 GB worth of documents, in 2007. Fortunately, the company was very methodical in how they named documents, and it became easy to understand which ones to focus on to achieve the greatest results.

Now imagine that you're able to fit the 20% most impactful

of your actions into a shorter period of time, and make it work. The concept in the following section will help understand how you can achieve this. And it's also how I managed to go through the documents in Cairo.

Parkinson's Law

"Work expands so as to fill the time available for its completion"
- Definition from Wikipedia

Parkinson's Law (one of my favorites) states that a task will use the time that you have allocated for it, not its scheduled time, but the time truly allocated for it. For example:

- Let's say you have to write a long essay due in **one month.** This would be the scheduled time. Being organized, you could distribute its completion over the course of four weeks, perhaps doing research the first week, then structuring your idea on the second week, writing the first draft on the third and doing final touches on the fourth. But in reality, if you're an average student like I was, then you'll probably find yourself pulling an all-nighter **one day before the deadline** (this would be the allocated time). If you then aced the essay with flying colors, your mistaken conclusion would be: "I work well under pressure". There are two reasons why I say it's mistaken:

1. High stress is pretty bad for productiveness; as we saw in Mindful vs. Stressed, the best state is somewhere in the middle.
2. If you had allocated more than one night to writing the essay you could have produced a much better result, and you would have probably learned a lot more. Getting A+ doesn't necessarily mean that you're learning properly.

Ok, you might be wondering why Parkinson's Law is relevant to becoming super-productive. By understanding yourself, you can allocate time more efficiently and achieve the same results in less time. For example, if you decide to check emails for half an hour, instead of two, you'll probably procrastinate less and finish the task accordingly. Or take my own example, I had one week to study and master what I couldn't in two months before that. Because I had no more time than that, it became the exact amount of time I needed to cover the material and improve my score in the knowledge test. You can make the most out of Parkinson's Law if you structure the way you allocate time. In the next section, we'll review the most popular ways of doing just that.

Pomodoro Technique and the Rule of 52/17

Francesco Cirillo developed The Pomodoro Technique in the late 1980s, and it consists in creating Working Intervals of 25 minutes and then taking a 5 minutes break, after which a new 25 minutes pomodoro would start. Normally, it is recommended to take a longer, 15-min break, after 4 "pomodori" (pomodori being the plural for pomodoro in Italian).

The Rule of 52/17 is very similar to the Pomodoro Technique, but it has a 52-min working interval followed by a 17-min break. This one may sound too arbitrary, but it actually comes from an observation of the top 10% most productive users of a time tracking app called DeskTime, as published by The Muse.

Both these concepts are valuable because studies have shown that we tend to lose focus and drop productivity if we sustain long periods of continuous work. So it is important to take regular breaks, and hopefully, do some physical activity like walking, to increase concentration by supplying more blood to the brain, as well as enhance our energy levels and work better.

I mentioned these two because they are popular in the productivity world, but you can experiment to find which work-rest time relation works best for you. Personally, I like 45 minutes of concentration before taking a 15 min break. Back in the day, when I was a smoker, I was taking the breaks to get my dose of nicotine, without knowing that these breaks (cigarettes aside) were helping me achieve better results at work. Just keep in mind that the Working interval should be free of distractions: not checking emails, social media, chats, casual conversations with co-workers, etc. We'll talk more about this when we get to the Time Management Chapter. For now, we'll discuss a bit further about the right state of mind to be successful in your goals, and specifically on how to become a lucky person. Hint: it has to do with your state of mind.

Becoming Lucky

> *"Luck is a matter of preparation meeting opportunity."*
> - Lucius Annaeus Seneca

A lot of people see luck as chance; something random that occurs with no apparent cause. I'm of a different persuasion. For me, and many others, "having good luck" is something that can be learned. This capacity of learning how to be lucky is backed by research carried out by Richard Wiseman, a Professor of the Public Understanding of Psychology at the University of Hertfordshire in the United Kingdom. I'll quote for you the punchline from an article he wrote on this:

"My research revealed that lucky people generate good fortune via four basic principles. (1) They are skilled at creating and noticing chance opportunities, (2) make lucky decisions by listening to their intuition, (3) create self-fulfilling prophesies via positive expectations, and (4) adopt a resilient attitude that transforms bad luck into good."

In other words:

1. **Step out of your comfort zone:** Be open minded so you can recognize opportunities, or create them.
2. **Listen to your gut:** Stay tuned with your intuition and factor that into your decision-making process.
3. **Think positively:** foster your positivity. This will allow you the confidence to jump at an opportunity. Also, it will make you more agreeable, which will increase social opportunities.
4. **Be persistent:** Once you've locked into your objective, stay strong-hearted until you reach the desired result.

Of course, this is not the type of luck that will make you win the lottery, it's the kind of luck that will get you better jobs, better deals, better partners, etc.

Coming back to my first work experience, some of my peers considered me lucky for being able to spend one week in Egypt to get my Canadian Visa to go to the training school, but it didn't happen all by chance; it wasn't an easy process, I had to do all by myself in Cairo, it was my first time in the country, and it was in the beginning of Ramadan, so definitely stepping out of my comfort zone. At the Canadian Embassy things got a bit complicated because I only had a two day window to get a visa that normally required 2 weeks to get, but I didn't give up and I stayed positive until the end, and after being rejected two times, by the end of the day I finally got my Canadian Visa stamped in my passport. So I could say my actions "made me lucky."

Do keep in mind that, no matter how much good comes your way, you won't be able to become lucky if you're demanding too much from yourself and others. We'll talk a little bit about this in the next section when we cover perfectionism, and how damaging it can be.

Perfectionism

"Have no fear of perfection - you'll never reach it."
- Salvador Dali

"Perfect is the enemy of good"
- Italian proverb

"A bridge doesn't eliminate a river, it just makes it easier to cross; the river stays, nonetheless, the same."
- David Suescun.

Remember the Pareto rule? Trying to reach 100% of anything is very inefficient and unrealistic. Not only that, perfectionism is a great source of frustration. Trying to achieve perfection is the easiest way to waste your time and accomplish nothing. Our goal here is to become super-productive; this means we need to overcome our inner drive for perfection and strive to work toward that 80% which will reap the biggest benefits with a fraction of the effort.

Usually, perfectionists are very critical about themselves. It doesn't matter how hard they try; it's never enough. Ask yourself if you relate with any of these statements:

1. People keep telling you that you have a good body, but you believe it's just something they say to make you feel better; because you believe you're not slim, or ripped, or normal enough?
2. Do you brush your teeth several times in a row?
3. Do you usually give up early on tasks you think you won't be able to complete with an immaculate result?
4. Do you spend a lot of time on tasks that others seem to finish a lot quicker?
5. Do you consider that if something isn't perfect, then it's just mediocre?

If you do relate to some, or all, I strongly suggest checking out the Bibliography & Additional References at the end of the book. It's important to mention here that we all have the ability to modify our behaviors; this doesn't necessarily mean we are changing who we are, our values and personality traits are very likely to stick with us for the rest of our lives. It's all about getting around the things that don't add value or make us happy.

This is what I had to do the week prior to my training school when I had to put some of the learning material aside so I could focus only on important topics. At the beginning, I was anxious because I thought that mastering EVERYTHING was the only way, but after letting go of that irrational need I realized that good enough was enough for me. If you can work with the idea that something good enough is all you need, that will get you into a healthy dynamic state of mind. But you will still need to push yourself out of your comfort zone if you want to become super productive. The next chapter will show you why, and not only that, you'll learn how it ultimately makes you happier as well.

The Flow State

"People who learn to control inner experience will be able to determine the quality of their lives, which is as close as any of us can come to being happy."
- Mihaly Csikszentmihalyi

During a happiness research, psychologist Mihaly Csikszentmihalyi found that people are happy when they experience "flow state." Paraphrasing his TED talk, we could describe psychological flow as the following:

1. You're completely immersed in an activity: Absolutely concentrated and focused on it.
2. You experience ecstasy by entering an alternative reality.
3. You have clarity: you know what needs to be done, and you do it, getting immediate feedback on your results.
4. You know the activity is achievable and that you have the required skills to carry it out.
5. You forget yourself; you feel like you're part of something bigger.
6. You are completely focused on the present moment and lose track of time.
7. Whatever the task is, it is so rewarding that it becomes worthy of doing for its own sake.

We can reach the state of flow when the activity is highly challenging and the skills required are above average. Pushing ourselves to this state enhances our productivity as we accomplish things we wouldn't otherwise be able to do. It helps us improve our skills and feel accomplished. Entering a flow state overlaps with "stepping out of the comfort zone"; if you keep doing something that doesn't represent a challenge or causes some discomfort, then you'll be doomed to a boring and uneventful life. And if you do challenge yourself, you'll also be conquering one of the factors that help you become lucky.

One of the first times I remember getting into a flow state was back in college. We had a coding group assignment to make a Minesweeper Game, in C+ and from scratch. For some reason I can't recall, we didn't do it, and we only had from 6 pm until 6 am to do it. We were three in the group, one gave up immediately after realizing that the odds were stacked up against us, but the other and I decided to at least try. We began by doing the welcome screen, and once we got a good looking one we started adding functionality line by line. Time flew by, and before we realized it was 5 am and the game was at 100% functionality! After this first experience, I was able to go into a flow state very often for different projects, but mostly writing and coding. This particular experience also illustrates Parkinson's Law.

To start putting all of the concepts and principles of super-productivity mentioned so far into practice, you will probably need some willpower. In the next section, we'll cover some important points about how to harness it.

Willpower and Its Limits

"I am, indeed, a king, because I know how to rule myself."
- Pietro Aretino

Willpower is defined by the Merriam-Webster Dictionary as "the ability to control yourself: (a) strong determination that allows you to do something difficult".

In the past, it used to be said that you either had willpower, or you didn't. Today we know that willpower can be nourished and replenished, much like a muscle, but as such, it can also be fatigued and exhausted. So, why is it important? Well, we use willpower throughout our day to resist the temptation of seeking things that give instant pleasure but are probably not aligned with our long-term goals. It is because of this that willpower plays a very important role in how we make decisions, and by over-using it, we expose ourselves to taking undesirable trade-offs when we're low on it. This process of making bad decisions when we have depleted our willpower is called "ego depletion", and we'll cover it in the next section.

To increase your willpower you can do a few things:
1. **Replace the need of willpower by creating habits:** When you act by habit you no longer need to take ego-depleting decisions.
2. **Outsource your willpower to others:** Let other people take decisions that aren't critical to you, for you.
3. **If you need to "focus" your willpower, let go of some of its other uses:** An example would be allowing yourself to eat treats on a binge day after "dieting" for a week.
4. **Be organized:** Disorganization destroys willpower; keep your workplace and tasks organized.

5. **Tackle one thing at a time:** Trying to juggle multiple things results in a faster ego depletion.

Some of the techniques we'll discuss in the chapters about managing habits, time & energy will help you foster your willpower as well. But it is important that we discuss a bit further about ego depletion before moving on to the next chapter, as this knowledge will help us understand the importance of creating habits.

Ego Depletion & Decision Paralysis

"I've always suspected that we start each day with a limited number of decision-making points that, once depleted, leave us cognitively impaired."
- Tim Ferriss

We briefly mentioned ego depletion before; once we have used up our willpower, we reduce our capacity to control ourselves. The big problem with ego depletion is that this gets in the way of our good judgment; some studies suggest we might become less ethical as we experience ego depletion. So, if making decisions causes ego depletion, and ego depletion causes us to make wrong decisions, then reducing the amount of decisions we have to take probably allows us to save our willpower for when it matters the most.

You may have noticed that highly productive people tend to stick to rituals in many aspects of their lives:
- Steve Jobs and Mark Zuckerberg always dressing the same
- Tim Ferriss always eating the same

I cited these examples because these are daily struggles for many of us:
- What to wear
- What to eat

When we face too many alternatives, we suffer decision paralysis (a.k.a analysis paralysis), meaning we have difficulties with making one decision. This paralysis happens partly due to our aversion to loss, which is one well known human characteristic. This aversion leads us to overthink the decision process and overrate the outcomes of the decision, to avoid loss. For example, deciding whether to have a beef or chicken burrito because you don't want to miss out on the tastiest meal can negatively add to our ego depletion while not creating a lot of value to our lives. Or while buying a home appliance we don't particularly care for, we might spend unnecessary time and energy comparing specs, or even comparing prices at different stores, all because we don't want to spend too much money, or because you want to make sure you get the most feature-loaded one "just in case" you might need an unusual feature one random day. But how can we avoid this? Some of the things you can practice to reduce this effect are:

1. **Decide before having to make the decision:** You could, for example, decide to go for the "mexican" version of whatever food you're having (mexican pizza, mexican crepe, mexican burger, etc.), or ask another one of whatever dish or drink your companion is having, or in fancier restaurants you could decide to go for the chef's recommendation. In clothing, you could organize your weekly wardrobe, or select it the night before.

2. **Avoid the decision completely:** you could choose to use only one clothing style, eat the same food continuously (same breakfast, same snacks, same lunch, and same dinners). If you're driving you could just take the route that Waze (or a similar GPS app) gives you, etc. It takes a subtle and complex mind to be single-mindedly determined.

And thus, we've reached the end of this chapter. We learned important concepts and principles that will help us stay motivated while learning new things. We've also learned how to set goals and prepare ourselves for success, not only by setting up things and environments but also our states of mind. Now we are armed with the fundamental principles that will aid us in our quest for super-productivity. And packed with all this valuable baggage, we'll move forward to learn how to create habits, which will allow us to implement all of this, and all that we have left to learn.

In a Blink

Let's review the main ideas of this chapter in a blink.

What drives Adults to learn?

According to Malcolm Knowles' principles of Andragogy, adults:

1. Are internally motivated and self-directed
2. Bring life experiences, and knowledge, to their learning experiences
3. Are goal oriented
4. Are relevancy oriented
5. Are practical
6. Like to be respected

By understanding what drives us to learn, we can change the way we approach our learning experiences and make the most out of them. This skill will be particularly useful to achieve great results with the topics we'll cover in the book.

Preparation

The first thing we'll have to start doing in our journey towards productivity involves setting goals. To do so, we've covered the technique known as S.M.A.R.T objectives, which states that objectives need to be Specific, Measurable, Achievable, Relevant, and Time-bounded. Once we have short and long term goals, we need to keep preparing by doing a "mise en place", and get the elements required for success available to us.

Mindful vs. Stressed?

Stress can be used to our advantage, but this will only work if we achieve a good balance between stress and relaxation.

The 80/20 Pareto Principle

So we know where we want to get, now we need to choose how to do so. The Pareto Principle will help us choose the best path. According to this principle, most of the results can be achieved with a small set of our actions. So by analyzing which actions create the biggest impact, we can focus on the right things to work on.

Parkinson's Law

Parkinson's Law explains that "Work expands so as to fill the time available for its completion". This phenomenon is useful for us because we can allocate shorter times to tasks that could normally eat our time, like emails, meetings, etc. And still manage to get them done properly, leaving us more free time to work on that 20% of things that will reap the 80% of benefits.

Pomodoro Technique and the 52/17

These time management techniques are ways to help us balance the focused and relaxed states of mind. Pomodoro consists of alternating 25 minutes of focused work with 5 minutes of break. And after completing 4 of these cycles taking a longer break of 15 minutes before starting a new cycle. The Rule of 52/17: It consists of a 52 minutes working interval followed by a 17-minute break. The main idea is to have set long intervals of work interspersed with set short intervals of rest to increase efficiency.

Becoming Lucky

By lucky I mean being the kind of person that seems to always get good deals out of situations where others usually get none. This is how to get lucky:

1. Step out of your comfort zone.
2. Listen to your gut.
3. Think positively.
4. Be persistent.

The Flow State

When you are in the flow state:

1. You're completely immersed in an activity.
2. You experience ecstasy by entering an alternative reality.
3. You have clarity.
4. You know the activity is achievable and that you have the required skills to carry it out.
5. You forget yourself.
6. You are completely focused on the present moment and lose track of time.
7. Whatever the task is, it is so rewarding that it becomes worthy of doing for its own sake.

We can reach flow state when the activity is highly challenging and the skills required are above average. Pushing ourselves to this state enhances our productivity as we accomplish things we wouldn't otherwise be able to do. It helps us improve our skills and feel accomplished.

Willpower and its limits

Willpower is our capacity to control ourselves, and it is like a muscle: It can get stronger but it also weakens after every use. It's important to have good reserves to avoid making bad decisions, and some of the things we can do to increase our willpower are:

1. Replace the need of willpower by creating habits.
2. Outsource your willpower to others.
3. If you need to "focus" your willpower let go of some of its other uses.
4. Be organized.
5. Tackle one thing at a time.

Ego depletion & Decision Paralysis

The exertion of our willpower is known as ego depletion, and it affects negatively our decisions and our ethics. Decision paralysis occurs when we get overwhelmed by having to make too many decisions leaving us idle to make any at all. To help us avoid these undesired states, we can do the things we already mentioned to increase our willpower and add the following:

1. Decide before having to make the decision.
2. Avoid the decision completely.

Chapter 3: Creating Habits

How This Chapter Came To Be

As you know by now, I've always loved learning new things. I quickly realized that I could only improve new skills through practice, repetition and taking on challenges. The best way to organize my skill-improving was through habits. So I made a habit of all the things I wanted in my life. This became an extremely useful trait when I started my job, as I was naturally inclined to analyze the processes involved in my tasks, and making routines that I could use for forming habits to be more productive and make time for other valuable things.

At that point habits and routines were one and the same. It was only when I finally quit smoking, after many failures over a decade of trying, that I understood that routines were only a part of the habits. This small bit of information may sound insignificant at first, but it is this little piece of information that allowed me to quit smoking after 16 years without recurring to sheer willpower, suffering withdrawal effects, ruining my social life, or gaining weight. I'll explain how in the first section of the chapter.

But that's only one of the many benefits of understanding habits, and how to create them. After quitting my job working in the field for almost 7 years, I got a new job in a management position as Service Delivery Manager for Gabon, Africa. I had to learn about the new company's culture, policies, standards, services, etc. After getting overwhelmed at the beginning of the assignment, I started forming new habits to help myself become more productive, we'll go through these habits in later chapters.

In this chapter, we'll have a quick look at the difference between habits and willpower, as well as how to create habits and some useful insight of how these can be used in learning environments to help you excel.

Habits vs. Willpower

If you didn't mindlessly read through the last chapter like a zombie, you learned that willpower gets depleted as we use it. If we have to rely completely on willpower to stick to our habits, we will lack willpower in other areas of our life where we might use it better. That's one of the reasons why we want to use habit creation as a strategy to becoming super-productive. In this book, you will learn techniques and tips that will aid you on your road to productivity. But just knowledge or awareness is not enough. Execution is the difference between zero and hero. The better prepared you are to start making these techniques part of your habits, the more likely you'll be to succeed in getting more out of life. Doing so will allow you to complete repetitive, taxing tasks faster and with less effort.

Habits (by which I mean 'good habits') are automated routines that get performed given certain stimuli and yield desired results. By creating habits we can automate part of our lives to become extremely productive. To understand how to create habits, we first need to dissect them. Four elements compose habits:

1. **The Cue**
2. **The Action**
3. **The Belief**
4. **The Reward**

So, the habit formula would be:

When "the cue" happens, the "action" (that is, a routine or behavior) is performed, which is expected to contribute to "the belief", and also allowing you to experience "the reward."

To give you a couple of examples:
- Before getting to bed (cue) I brush my teeth (action) to avoid getting cavities, gum decease, etc. (Belief), and then I hit the sack with a minty fresh sensation in my mouth (reward).
- Right before starting my workout routine (cue) I perform a series of dynamic warm-up exercises (action) to avoid injuries (belief), and as a result, of the increased blood circulation/oxygenation, I feel more energized to do my actual workout routine (reward).

The belief and reward parts appear to be very similar. If you google "How to create habits" you'll find that most authors and references are to 3 elements only, only citing the reward. Think of the belief as a long term reward or goal, with no immediate feedback, and the reward as the instantaneous positive feedback you get, which motivates you right then and there. It's important to get the difference clearly, as the short-term rewards for good and bad habits are usually "good", but long term reward is only "good" for good habits and "punishing" for the bad ones (like getting overweight, cancer, etc.).

Going back to when I quit smoking; by understanding habits, I understood that I didn't have to turn my life upside down and change all the habits in my life that I had already associated with smoking: coffee breaks with my peers, having a couple of drinks during the weekend, taking some time out in heated arguments, etc. I understood that I only needed to slightly modify the routine (by simply not smoking) and still get the benefits of building friendships at work, taking breaks between focused work intervals, enjoy a beer or two without having to get out of the bar every hour, taking time out to breathe and cool my mind in heated situations and so on. I didn't change my habits, I only modified them. This was how I quit smoking without having to resort to sheer willpower, and without withdrawal symptoms, gaining weight or messing up my social and working life, by changing the routine (action) part of the equation in the smallest of details: a lit cigarette going to my mouth, and keeping the rewards from my habits intact.

And now that you know what comprises a habit, we'll go through the steps you can follow to succeed at habit creation.

How to Create Habits

"Make it so easy you can't say no."
- Leo Babauta

To create new habits, first you have to choose the habit and the right cue, then get the momentum to do the action, define the belief and the reward, and remember to be forgiving and persistent. These are the steps in a little more detail:

Step 1: Choose the habit you want to incorporate in your life

First decide on something that will help you improve your life, your work, your study, whatever, and then you can make a habit out of it. It could be a small habit (like starting to floss) or a big one (like picking up a new language). Either way, you'll need to judge what you want to work on given your needs and desires. If there is more than one area where you would like to improve, it is important to understand that habit creation is better done one habit at a time. If you try to juggle more things than you can handle, you'll probably end up dropping all of them.

Be patient.

Step 2: Choose the right cue

It is much easier to recycle some of the elements from the habits we already have. It is easier to stick to "working out", or whatever habit you want to incorporate, right after arriving from work, rather than at an arbitrary time of day, like "at 6 pm" (or any given hour). Choosing the best cues is very important, as they are the beginning of it all. If you select something that has a high chance of occurring, then you're one step closer to actually starting to get things done.

It is good to schedule new habit creation around recurrent events like waking up, before/after taking a shower, before/after breakfast, before/after work, etc. These things happen almost every day for most of us.

It doesn't have to be time-bounded only, the cue could be someone, somewhere or even when you experience a certain emotion; like complementing your significant other when you see them.

Step 3: Get momentum to do the action

If the action you want to have in your habit is very pleasant, it will probably be easier to start doing it. But let's assume it is something that pushes you out of your comfort zone. What I'm about to say may sound silly, but the best way to start is actually starting. Once you start the action or behavior, you're very likely to get a sense of discomfort, something very similar to pain. This pain is the reason we usually fail at sticking to new habits. To combat this, you'll need two elements: a. willpower and b. being able to re-frame the situation. Willpower will help you take the first steps and start gaining some momentum. You also need a constant "catch phrase" to keep yourself going, so you can re-frame that situation of discomfort as: "I could be doing X, but I chose to do Y because I know this is what I need to do to get me to Z".

When starting a habit, it is important to start at a difficulty level you feel comfortable with and find it difficult to talk yourself out of doing your routine. You can start increasing the difficulty/performance as your habit gets stronger.

Step 4: Define the belief

If you have a strong, solid belief system you can hold on to, you will increase your chances of actually acquiring the habit. It is important that the belief system you choose is right for you. It needs to have a direct, positive impact on your life. To continue using the workout analogy:

Bad Belief System: I want to work out, so others will find me sexier and more desirable.

Good Belief System: I want to work out so I can get stronger, suffer less pain, enjoy outdoor activities more, and live healthier and longer.

If you are aiming to please others over your own needs, you won't get far. In the example above, a side effect of the good belief is that you'll have a better body and others will notice, but that shouldn't be why you do it.

You can use your belief as the catch phrase you internalize to keep you going during the 'action' execution.

Step 5: Define the reward

Sometimes the immediate reward is not apparent, so you need to be creative and look for the silver lining. If you're exercising, the reward could be a simple "Clap-clap" (Freeletics, a workout app, uses this, and it works wonders). For me, the reward is being all sweaty at the end, because that's when the endorphins of reward feeling are flooding my brain. It could also be a mental shout, like "I rule!"

You have to find a reward that engages positive emotion. The reward is something immediate, or short-termed, so you can modify the reward as you go, to sustain a healthy habit cycle.

Step 6: Be forgiving

Creating a new habit is no easy task. It requires planning, discipline, and most of the time, actual work. Be forgiving to yourself if you slip every now and again. Don't let a mistake be the end of you, remember why you started to work on getting that new habit to begin with.

Step 7: Be persistent

Creating a new habit takes time. Every time you run through the habit cycle, you get closer to engraving it into your brain.

In 1960, Maxwell Maltz, a plastic surgeon, published the book Psycho-Cybernetics where he mentioned an observation he had made regarding his patients: he observed that **it would take a minimum of 21 days for his patients to start getting used to the transformation they had undertaken**. This observation was popularized as: "it takes 21 days to create a habit". The problem is that this short period of time might be too hopeful, and following this generalization could prove discouraging, plus it's clearly missing the "a minimum of" part of the statement.

In 2009, Phillippa Lally, a health psychology researcher at University College London, published a study in the European Journal of Social Psychology, where the research team followed the habit creation patterns of 96 volunteers. The habits would vary in difficulty, and the study was conducted for 12 weeks (84 days). The model they came up with shows that it could take from 18 to 254 days to make a habit automatic.

It is good to keep in mind that habits are good for you even when they are still being formed, before becoming automatic. This is how I transformed my workweek in a matter of two months: by slowly incorporating new habits.

The whole process before it became automatic took me six months (including the 2-months transition time), but in the end, I was very pleased as I had finally included working out into my working days. Before, I was always using the "I'm too tired to exercise" excuse to talk myself out of working out. That improvement was possible because I was leaving the office on time, not working on weekends, sleeping better, and other goodies you'll learn more about later in the book. So don't get held up on the time required. Concentrate on being persistent and keep in mind that missing one or two times is ok, and expected. Remember what we covered in the section on perfectionism, back in the chapter on key concepts and principles.

In the next section, we'll go through some specific habits that can be of great service when learning new things.

Habits For Learning Better

This section is interesting and deep enough to be a book by itself, and that's why we're only going to have a quick look at things you can work on to learn better, by using habits. Learning is something that impacts every aspect of our lives. The mere fact that you are reading this is a proof of your willingness and desire to learn. Learning helps you incorporate things that you are passionate about, or that you need to make life better, so this section goes to workers, students, and long-life learners all the same. The following is a compilation of advice that comes mainly from two great books on the subject, "A Mind For Numbers", by Barbara Oakley and "Learn More, Study Less" by Scott H. Young.

1. **Do not cram study material:** Whenever studying, cramming up material is counterproductive and doesn't yield positive results.

2. **Review material before going to sleep:** There are studies that suggest that the last things you experienced in a day, are more likely to be in your dreams, so this would allow you to "study while sleeping". Also, there's another study that suggests our brains review all our short term memories when we sleep, to move important things to long-term memory. It starts from the last thing that took place on your day and works itself backwards to the first; so you'll increase the chances of moving those memories to long term if they are the last thing you go through on your day.

3. **Chunk information:** Break down knowledge into pieces. By doing so, your brain is better prepared to join information and complete the missing gaps, so you don't need to know every little thing, but the main components, or chunks, of your subject.

4. **Recall the study material:** Try to retrieve the main ideas from your memory regularly. Try remembering the ideas and concepts, instead of just re-reading material.

5. **Do not highlight text:** This, along with re-reading, is deceiving and time-consuming. When you go through it, you have the false sensation of understanding, just because it's familiar to you. So you can finish a study session erroneously thinking you have it locked in your brain.

6. **Focus on the process instead of the product:** This will help avoid procrastination. If you concentrate in the result, you'll see yourself so far away from it that it will be easy to give up. Focus on the process of learning, this will allow you to judge yourself less harshly.

7. **Use different venues to study:** Since we are animals of habit, studying in the same place also tricks the mind and pushes it into the familiar, deceiving part of the study session. By changing the environment, you'll allow your brain to explore new pathways to access the desired knowledge, thus strengthening the memory and retention.

8. **Plan for play:** When you're scheduling to study, you might stress about it. It is important to plan for play, and allow yourself, and your brain, to relax.

9. **Make information memorable by making it visual:** This is a well-known technique of making funny, outrageous mnemonics and turns of phrase, as the brain will be more likely to remember those.

10. **Use metaphors to simplify concepts:** This will let you piggy back ride from other concepts that you are familiar with or that you already understand.

11. **Test your knowledge regularly:** This facilitates learning, thanks to the so-called testing effect. A study concluded that when participants are regularly tested, they performed better than a group that only used their time for study (without being tested). Even if the tests results while studying were poor.

12. **Use spaced repetitions:** Spaced repetitions are repetitions of the thing you want to learn, not in quick succession, and not with a very long time in between, but with just enough temporal spacing for the short term memory to be weaker. Joining recalling, retrieving and testing the material, you can structure these habits with spaced repetitions, which have the added value of making you recall information right before you forget it, increasing the chances of moving it into long term memory. The easiest way of doing this is using flashcards or apps like Memrise or Anki. The advantage of Anki is that it offers a vast repository of community contributed stacks of cards on a myriad of topics, automatizing the spaced repetition. My preferred method is Memrise, it is a lot friendlier; it's a systematic way of using flashcards to learn, especially for learning languages. It uses the space repetitions algorithms to grow your knowledge, and it allows you to choose mnemonics to learn better.

As I mentioned before, this is just a brief overview of how habits can help you achieve more by helping you learn better.

And so we end this chapter, where we learned about the parts that constitute habits and the steps we can take to build them. This knowledge will be the cornerstone of your success in acquiring the techniques we'll learn in the following chapters. We'll start with Time Management.

In a Blink

Let's review the main ideas of this chapter in a blink.

Habits vs. Willpower

Habits are a key element of becoming super productive, as they allow you to perform taxing tasks in a more effective manner. The four elements that compose habits are:

1. The Cue
2. The Action
3. The Belief
4. The Reward

They connect into the habit formula like this: When "the cue" happens, the "action" gets executed, which is expected to contribute to "the belief", and allows you to experience "the reward."

How to Create Habits

In order to successfully create habits, you can follow these steps:

1. Choose the habit you want to incorporate in your life
2. Choose the right cue
3. Get momentum to do the action
4. Define the belief
5. Define the reward
6. Be forgiving
7. Be persistent

You shouldn't place too much importance in how long it takes to build a habit, you should place more importance on being persistent instead.

Habits for learning better

The following are some excellent habits that can help you improve your learning efforts:

1. Do not cram study material.
2. Review material before going to sleep.
3. Chunk information.
4. Recall the study material.
5. Do not highlight text.
6. Focus on the process instead of the product.
7. Use different venues to study.
8. Plan for play.
9. Make information memorable by making it visual.
10. Use metaphors to simplify concepts.
11. Test your knowledge regularly.
12. Use spaced Repetitions.

This is an example of how habits can be applied to learning.

Chapter 4: Time Management

How This Chapter Came To Be

When someone mentions productivity, we almost immediately think about Time Management and wonder how we can achieve more in less time. To help you get some quick wins, we'll cover techniques that will help you improve your time management.

While working in the oil field it was very clear for me what needed to be done, and the time to do it was limited by external factors, so it was "easy" and mandatory to be ready to execute our services when the time came. Any deviation from that meant a fault in service delivery, and I was responsible and accountable for it. When I started moving upwards in the corporate ladder, and I was given roles in middle management and sales & marketing, the tasks were blurred, and immediate results were not the main focus of the role. Long term goals were the priority, and that change of mindset took a while to set in. At first, I was trying to tackle the tasks in the same way I was doing my field work, which in my opinion was highly optimized to be as effective as I could manage, but that didn't work out well for me; it is impossible to finish all the tasks because they constantly need feedback from clients, internal customers, marketing strategies, etc.

Time management became imperative for me because I was working very long hours and never seeing the end of it. The praise from my boss at that time was very positive, I was doing what was expected and then some, but in a very unsustainable manner for me. That assignment lasted 2 months. After a couple of months back in the field, I was given the opportunity to work in operations management for field ops. I had learned my lesson, and started using my time management techniques to work in my favor, and since my knowledge and experience in field ops was ample, I skipped a huge part of the learning curve. But sometimes you have to suck up and stick with the learning curve, and time management plays a good part in being able to fit in time for training and self-actualization, very important tasks that shouldn't be overlooked.

We'll go through some techniques that are easy to follow, and have amazing results if you work hard to implement them. We'll start from a familiar place: To-do-List-landia.

The To-do lists

"It seems essential, in relationships and all tasks, that we concentrate only on what is most significant and important."
- Soren Kierkegaard

In this chapter, we will see some of the concepts we've already covered implemented into concrete actions. But before doing so, let's go through a couple of new concepts that will help keep it all together.

To-do lists are the most common time management technique used in any workplace. They are very intuitive and can easily be done on paper or digitally. But just because a lot of people use them it doesn't mean they are always effective, or productive. For a lot of people, to-do lists turn into an endless list of things that might never get done. We also get lazy with them, and sometimes write down things that we later can't even figure out why they're there to begin with. But with all their flaws, done properly they can be of great service. The following rules will help you get your To-do lists right:

1. **Jot down as many things as you want:** Write down a lot of things on lists, mainly to keep your mind from wandering too much. If something catches your attention, write it down to review it later.

2. **Review and organize the lists:** You can use a notepad and pen, or apps like Evernote,   GTasks or Trello to write your lists.   Once a week you should clean them out to remove what is no longer relevant, and to categorize the remaining items; you may have to-do lists for daily tasks, music, movies & books, ideas to explore, and business projects.

Having these categories allows you to prioritize the tasks.

3. **Write them as actionable items:** Just writing a keyword or reference is not enough. Try to write items as clear actions with time requirements and details.

4. **If it is something that you can do in 2 minutes or less, do it straight away:** There's no point in collecting tasks. If there's an item that you can do right then and there, just do it.

5. **Write daily lists (MITs):** Do them by the end of each day to have a clear purpose the next day, try to write no more than 3-5 MITs, a.k.a Most-Important-Things. Lists longer than that won't get done. The MITs are the minimum things you need to do to achieve a productive day.

6. **Make the most difficult task the first:** If you leave the most difficult tasks for the end of the day, you'll have ego depletion and will end up pushing the task for the next day, day after day, thus procrastinating. So eat your frogs first!

And an added value of using lists to capture things that catch your attention, is that you can see trends of things that regularly appear on your lists, hinting you into a direction of something that excites you, or interests you, which can be used for new businesses, to explore new careers, to know yourself better, etc.

A variation of the daily to-do lists are follow-up lists. These lists allow you to follow up on unfinished or recurring tasks. I would use this often to remind myself to ask for updates in procurement orders, something that could normally take months from placing an order to receiving the goods, or any other task that couldn't be completed in one go. I used to do this on an Excel Sheet, and I would set a follow-up reminder with varying periodicities (once per week, once per month, every three months or every six months). You can download it from http://deft.xyz/1UfTnpO, but you could also explore some other alternatives like Workboard (http://www.workboard.com/), Asana (https://asana.com/) or Trello (https://trello.com/). These web services allow you to organize tasks within teams, which results in eliminating a lot of unnecessary emails. Be advised that these systems require the "team" to be willing to use those systems, so if you're a lone wolf on this one you're better off using a To-Do app with time calendar scheduling, like Todoist, or something similar to my Excel system.

You can also have to-do lists for repetitive tasks, for example, a good to-do list to go through in the mornings is the following:

- Meditate,
- reflect in gratitude,
- set your daily intention (mind your MITs),
- pad your schedule (plan for play),
- hydrate (drink water),
- stretch (yoga, or similar),
- listen to music,
- smile,
- clean up after yourself,
- do your hardest task first (eat your frogs first).

But creating tasks is all too easy, and if you don't manage them well they can lead to busywork. That's why it's important to set some restrictions and rules on things we shouldn't do, and that's exactly what we'll review in the next section.

The Not-to-do List

> *"... What you don't do determines what you **can** do."*
> - Tim Ferriss

The first time I heard about this concept was from Tim Ferriss' blog. I have to agree completely with Tim on not-to-do lists being more effective than to-do lists. A not-to-do list is a set list of things that you commit to not doing. My list goes as follows:

1. Do not use notifications on your phone:
I don't have any audible or vibrating notifications on my phone. The reason: It is very distracting and constantly disconnects me from what I'm doing, or from the person I'm sharing time with. If it is an important communication, people will call, so don't worry about missing out.

2. Do not check email at bed:
I don't check emails first thing in the morning; I do this to avoid de-railing from **my priorities** and not letting others push theirs into my day. I also avoid reading emails before sleeping for two reasons: 1. If I get my mind working I won't be able to fall asleep, and 2. blue light, which comes from back-lit devices like mobiles, tablets or computers, inhibits the production of melatonin in the brain, which will make sleeping more difficult because it messes up the natural circadian rhythm.

3. Do not stress over low-impact problems:
You can tell the size of a man by the size of things that bother him. Whenever a problem arises, I inspect it to determine if it's worth my time. If the problem at hand is low-impact or unimportant, I delegate it and forget about it. If I can't delegate, I don't deal with it as if it

were urgent. We will elaborate on this later in this chapter when we discuss How to Prioritize.

4. **Do not engage in negativity-filled conversations:**

This kind of conversations are very taxing on energy; normally, they are promoted by energy vampires that will suck the life out of you if you let them.

If it's a conversation that you can't avoid, for example if a subordinate needs to vent, then try to flip the tone of the conversation: ask the person what he/she (not you) can do to improve the situation? And if it's above their area of influence, then ask what you can do so he/she can move on.

5. **Do not consume media aimlessly:**

I don't watch, listen or read the news. I don't go browsing the web to find material to consume either. The news are generally very negative, and most of the time don't add value to my life. Also, if it is something important, most of the people talk about it, so I still get informed of events that might impact me.

For the media to read and watch, I usually pick from curated sources, like Pocket's Recommendations, Farnam Street, Tim Ferriss Blog, etc. We will come back to this point in the chapter on information management.

6. **Do not multitask:**

When I was a teenager, multitasking was considered to be linked with more productivity, so I was a heavy multitasker. I know now that multitasking is awful for productivity, so I need to remind myself not to multitask. We'll discuss this further in the next section.

This not-to-do list was very beneficial for me when I moved from the field to the office. This set list allowed me to draw the line, respect my private time, and keep my work from spilling all over my non-work time. I started re-connecting with my friends and family as I stopped being a slave of my smartphone. Overall, it helped me calm down, which in return allowed me to make better decisions, sleep better and be happier. Try making your own list and keep it visible to remind you to stick to it!

Work on a Single Task

> *"Most of the time multitasking is an illusion. You think you are multitasking, but in reality you're actually wasting time switching from one task to another."*
> - Bosco Tjan

There's an overwhelming amount of studies that have concluded that multitasking is terrible for productivity, to the point that it may account for 40% of productivity loss. Our brain doesn't have the capacity to work on more than one thing at a time, so when we claim to "multitask", we are really switching between tasks. A study concluded that for our brains to fully recover the lost concentration after switching tasks, it takes an average time of 23 minutes. For example, by doing two 20 minutes tasks in "multitasking" mode, it could take up to 1 or 1.5 hours, instead of the 40 minutes it would take if you only do one task first, and then the other.

Part of the problem is that we feel we are productive while multitasking, so we get a stimulating dopamine release as a reward, which reinforces the bad habit of multitasking. As a reminder for yourself, the not-to-do list has a focus on avoiding multitasking.

So, what is the alternative? -> Single-Tasking!

When you allow yourself to focus entirely on one thing, you can properly maximize the efficiency of your brain power, and you're more likely to produce good results in the fastest possible way. Remember the Pomodoro and the 52/17 Techniques? Single-tasking is the perfect scenario to utilize them. Have your daily MITs, and use the concept behind "The ONE Thing": which is "*Find ONE thing that you can do, that if done will make all the other things easier, or unnecessary*", to decide what things you'll devote your time to. Working on a single task also helps you enter the "flow state", a state where you lose yourself, fully focused, and make the most out of your skills, ultimately making you happier and more productive.

The biggest challenges to single-tasking:

Single-tasking might still be perceived as not being very productive, due to the false myths surrounding multitasking. So for a while, until single-tasking becomes the new norm, you might need to explain to others what you are doing. Explain to them how damaging interruptions are, and that it's not ok to constantly interrupt you to ask for things that aren't truly important and urgent. We'll discuss a bit further on communicating with others in the chapter on communication management.

Other ways of letting people know that you are not constantly available are:

1. **Use headphones and find the music that pushes your focus forward:** People are less willing to interrupt you if they have to touch you or signal you.

2. **When someone interrupts, raise your hand to signal them that you are busy and just keep working on whatever you're working:** If the task on hand has a long way to go, then stop and inquire what the interruption is about.

3. **Practice saying No:** It is very tempting to be helpful and say "yes" to every minimal request everybody does. But this is very harmful, as you're constantly leaving **your priorities** unattended to help others. Saying yes to all the requests you get

depletes your energy, and ultimately, people are not all that appreciative of your extra efforts.

4. **Trust and Delegate**: This is a hard one. If you can't let go of some control, then people will always need to run things through you, creating constant interruptions. The best way to reframe this is like this: If you ever want to grow out of your role, you'll need someone to take over your current activities, so don't feel threatened by coaching others on them. Another perk of trusting others is that everything becomes easier and faster, plus you benefit emotionally from the optimistic mindset as it adds positive feelings that help your happiness levels.

Every change requires patience, if you let others know that you are changing the way you work, they won't get offended by your newly acquired focus. The four ways of letting others know that you're busy working on some focused task work pretty well in both open and closed office environments. I tried them, and they are particularly useful in an open office as there's a common tendency for peers to walk by for quick chats that end up extending over long periods, contrary to close offices where you can easily close the door to signal people that you're unavailable. After I had made it clear to all my teamwork that I was working single-tasking, I started shaving off hours from my workday. I even started clearing tasks from upcoming days with scheduled/delayed emails and allowing myself to work on "big picture" tasks. My peers didn't resent me, as I was scheduling time to tend to their needs, so I was actually spending better quality time with my team.

In fact, you can use single tasking in combination with time-restriction techniques (like pomodoros), to make the most out of your time. Let's see how.

Batching Tasks

Batching tasks means grouping similar tasks and working on them in batches. This concept is not new, and it's commonly used in operations management as an integral part of maximizing production. Whenever there is a task, there is a preparation required to do so (mise en place). For instance, you set up a time, place or event to start doing it. By batching tasks by similarity, you utilize the set-up time for multiple purposes, instead of having to set-up multiple times, again and again, wasting valuable time and energy. The activity batching will greatly differ from job to job. But there are still some things that are universal:

1. **Batch email reading/writing:** Instead of constantly opening your email client, or email tab, or checking your smartphone, dedicate one or two windows a day where you check your emails. In my case, 1.5 hours after I started my work day was a good time to run the first batch. Whenever I read an email that requires my input, I hit reply and close the reply window, leaving a draft behind. After finishing my email reading batch, I start my email writing one, and I go through the drafts to make sure I send my replies.

2. **Batch reporting:** If you have to write or read reports, do not do that as they come, batch the whole process and allocate a part of your day to do it. In my case, I used to designate one day a week for this purpose.

3. **Batch expenses once a month:** If you have expenses that you can claim (work or benefits), do them once a month.

4. **Batch Cooking:** Over the last year I was living mostly by myself, having to make myself breakfast, lunch, dinner and snacks all by myself for the first time in my life. I started doing batch-cooking by preparing freezable meals and then using them throughout the week. There are plenty of recipes out there; I would normally do Indian Dal, Black, and Red beans, spice beef/chicken/fish and portion it meal-sized. Rice, pasta, and stews are also common in batch cooking.

5. **Batch dish washing:** For me washing dishes, although a dreaded chore, is kind of relaxing. But it becomes a nightmare if I have to do it regularly. So I only do the dishes once a day, at the end of the day. The setup gain isn't too much because it's just putting some gloves on, but I batch it more for energy conservation purposes.

6. **Batch clothes washing, folding and ironing:** I usually do my laundry on Sunday evening and fold and organize everything at night. If you split whites and color, you might need two days to do this, unless you have access to multiple washing machines and can do them at the same time.

The last three points refer to activities you can outsource. But that strongly depends on the cost and ease of hired domestic work in your country.

In general, batching can be tailored to specific groups of tasks. These tasks don't have to share an identical subject, topic, activity, etc. But they have to share similarities (in skills and set up required). If you are a writer, you could set mornings for book writing and evenings for blog posts. If you are a teacher, it might be preparing classes, going through tests, etc. Find what works best for you and schedule yourself. Pomodoro (and other time-restricted techniques) are great for task batching as well. You can also apply Parkinson's law (making work fit into the time allotted for it) when batching, assigning short periods of time to push yourself to go through the batches more effectively.

This is also where schedules work best: I had a fixed schedule to go through every week, with monthly, quarter, half year and yearly events noted down and accounted for. My schedule included time lots for working on my MIT's and daily to-do's, as well as all the other usual suspects: emails, meetings, reports, and follow-ups. Also, schedule the time for you to leave the office! Remember Parkinson's law, if you allocate time for work, you'll find yourself finishing on time, or even before the whistle blows (which should bring back some Flintstones memories to some).

There's something we haven't covered yet and it will make a great difference in how you spend your time: How to Prioritize. This topic is the priority of the next section.

How to Prioritize

"The key is not to prioritize what's on your schedule, but to schedule your priorities."
- Stephen Covey

It is extremely easy to say "prioritize". Doing so, not so easy. This difficulty exists because there's no easy one-size-fits-all approach on how to do this. The following guidelines will give you some structure to help you prioritize:

1. **Ask yourself what is the ONE thing:** Find ONE thing that you can do, that if done will make all the other things easier, or unnecessary. That one thing should probably be on the top of your priorities. Using Pareto analysis can help you reach this one thing from a systematic approach.

2. **Establish ranking criteria:** This will allow you to assess what truly matters for you. This criterion could be life-long for some things or a particular one-time thing for specific needs. For example, you could decide who to spend time and energy on, by having some criteria to determine who is worthy of it. You could also draft criteria when buying a house, and rank the features as per your desires and needs: number of rooms, square footing, patio, etc. Once you list the choices, you can just organize them using your rank.

3. **Use a matrix to sort tasks:** Use Eisenhower's method of arranging tasks by urgency and importance in a matrix or table, like this.

	Important	Not important
Urgent		
Not urgent		

You put *Urgency* on one axis and *Importance* on the other. Important activities are the ones that lead us toward our goals. Urgent activities require immediate attention, these lead towards someone else's goals. We usually waste a lot of time on these, commonly called "Fire Fighting" activities. So you end up with four quadrants, with different levels of priorities. Your priorities should go, from top to bottom, as follows:

- Important and urgent
- Important but not urgent
- Not important but urgent
- Not important and not urgent
4. **Use the MoSCoW method:** This a method usually applied to software development under the Agile methodology of project management, but can be adapted to other project management needs, especially informal ones. It consists in arranging activities under the following:

- Must Have
- Should Have
- Could Have
- Won't Have This Time

You could then decide how much time to spend working on each of those categories.

Overall, prioritizing is closely related to your goals. Having clear definitions of success is of paramount importance to proper prioritizing.

Activity Tracking

"What gets measured gets managed."
- Peter Drucker

If you know how you're spending your work time, then you can make decisions on changes that will help you reach your desired productivity level. There are apps, software and web services that allow you to "check in" to track a given activity.

There are also services that automatically track your "screen" activity; I use RescueTime for this purpose. You can define what activities are productive and which ones aren't (Facebook, scheduling, etc.). The best thing for me is that it runs in the background in all my devices simultaneously (computer, smartphone, and tablet) and it sends me a weekly report on Sundays to let me know my percentage of productive screen time and whether I've reached my desired goals. This tool is very powerful to look into your habits and maybe realize that you're derailing from your objectives, or on the contrary, give you positive feedback on how well you've been doing. On a side note to this resource, there are also services that let you block websites and apps for given periods of time to help you stay focused and distractions-free. StayFocusd is an example resource to do this. If apps and web services are not your thing, making handwritten notes is an equally valid way of tracking your activities to understand how you spend your time, and by doing so find where your troublesome areas rest. The same principle stays true: what doesn't get measured, doesn't get managed.

And with this, we've reached the end of the Time Management chapter. You've learned how to use To-do lists to your advantage, the importance of having a Not-to-do list, and why multitasking works against your productivity, and you'll hopefully start prioritizing your high impact tasks and work on them in batches, while single-tasking. In the next chapter, we'll discuss Energy Management, and how all aspects of your life play a role in how energized you are.

In a Blink

Blink twice if you're ready. Hey, what are you doing! This is called "In a Blink", not "In Two Blinks". Focus, dammit!

To-do lists

To-Do lists can be very beneficial if used correctly. Some basic rules to follow when creating to-dos:

1. Jot down as many things as you want.
2. Review and organize the lists.
3. Write them as actionable items.
4. If you can do it straight away, better just do it.
5. Write daily priority lists (MITs).
6. Make the most difficult task the first.

Aside from these, you can use a variation I call follow-up lists, with different calendar periodicities.

The Not-to-do List

A not-to-do list is a set list of things that you commit to not doing, which in turn allows you to focus on the important things. Here's my list:

1. Do not use notifications on your phone
2. Do not check email at bed
3. Do not stress over low-impact problems
4. Do not engage in negativity-filled conversations
5. Do not consume media aimlessly
6. Do not multitask

Work on a Single Task

Multitasking is actually counterproductive, and it affects negatively your productivity and mental sharpness. A better way of working is focusing on a single task. You can try some of the following to overcome the challenges of multitasking:

1. Use headphones.
2. When someone interrupts, let them know you're busy.
3. Practice saying No and avoid others from pushing their agendas on your own agenda.
4. Trust and Delegate to avoid task-checking interruptions.

Batching Tasks

Combining to-do's and single tasking you can create batches of similar tasks to work on them more effectively. Some of the things you can batch are:

1. Email reading/writing.
2. Reporting.
3. Expenses once a month.
4. Cooking.
5. Dish washing.
6. Clothes washing, folding and ironing.

Create batches that meet your work needs and particulars. And after doing so, you can organize them on your weekly schedule.

How to Prioritize

1. Ask yourself what is the ONE thing.
2. Establish ranking criteria.
3. Use a matrix to sort tasks (Like the Eisenhower matrix, having Urgency on one axis and Importance on the other).

4. Use the MoSCoW method (categorizing tasks into Must Have, Should Have, Could Have and Won't Have This Time)

Activity Tracking

To better manage how you spend your time, you need to measure and understand your current activities. You can do this with the good ol' pen, paper, and clock, or use apps like RescueTime. Once you have a clear idea of how you spend your time, you can make decisions on what to modify to reach your desired productivity level.

Chapter 5: Energy Management: Fuel Your Body & Mind

How This Chapter Came To Be

Do you remember being young, energetic, full of strength to take on the impossible? I bet you do! While growing up one tends to think that those conditions will last forever, regardless of what parents, teachers, uncles, and aunties say.

There also comes a time in our young adulthood, for some of us, where we catch ourselves thinking: "I think I'm getting too old for this." For me, that started becoming a very frequent line of thought, and I started to get worried because I had let myself slip away without even realizing it; I was overweight, I wasn't sleeping well, waking up in the morning was a dreadful task, I was getting stressed over small things, etc. I wasn't becoming the person I envisioned myself to be.

For me, work had a lot to do with this situation. My work required me to work long hours, sometimes as long as two days without sleep, managing service teams and being in charge of safety and quality. The food was provided by either the company or the clients, and in the Middle East it involves a huge amount of rice, small portions of veggies and lots of mutton and chicken. This started the poor sleeping and eating habits, and it only got worse when I was on time off, as I felt entitled (given my hard work), to party and eat like an animal. But this wasn't the worse part! Given my sleeping, eating and smoking habits, I was always short of energy and breath to do any kind of exercise.

For me, the lack of physical activity started with college, but I was constantly nostalgic for my skating years, or when I used to play tennis, etc. Also, in my teen years, I was interested in tantric sex, which involved a lot of theories on energy flow through the body and breathing techniques, and those good practices were also lost for me.

After quitting my field job, I had no real reason not to work on changing those things I didn't like about my life, and I started by quitting smoking and learning French, things I'd wanted to do for the longest of times. I also started to exercise again, something I had tried in the past but was difficult for me given that I have fibromyalgia (pain in several joints and parts of my body). I started pushing away negative elements in my life and started replacing them with more positive and fulfilling things.

All of this led me to have more energy, something that helped me a lot in the job I got as Service Delivery Manager. It was that extra energy that allowed me to adopt good habits and be more productive while getting more out of my personal life.

In this chapter, you'll learn how to manage your energy through everyday practices, and how these equate to productivity and happiness.

The Pillars

> *"Energy and persistence conquer all things."*
> - Benjamin Franklin

Managing one's energy is probably the most important part of becoming super productive, it will allow you to live a better, more enjoyable life as well.

In the Harvard Business Review (HBR) article "Manage Your Energy, Not Your Time", by Tony Schwartz & Catherine McCarthy, the authors break down energy management into four different areas. I like to refer to them as the four energy pillars, and these are:

1. **Body**
2. **Emotion**
3. **Mind**
4. **Spirit**

Let's go through each one and discuss their properties and how they add value to our objectives.

1. Body:

This pillar refers to our basic needs: the physical ones. It can be boiled down to breathing, eating, sleeping, and body movement. Much of how we feel comes from these essential activities. Our biochemistry is continuously changing to adapt to the stimuli we put our bodies through.

In this chapter, we'll cover these needs, and you'll learn how to improve your Body Energy.

2. Emotion:

This pillar refers to the polarity of your energy: positive or negative. The six basic emotions are joy, surprise, sadness, fear, disgust, and anger. You could say that joy and surprise are positive, and sadness, fear, disgust, and anger are negative, but actually they are all positive in that they are all useful evolutionary adaptations. What could be negative or positive about them is the lack of regulation (too much or too little of any of them). I'll refer to negative emotions as the unregulated ones.

Several studies have reached the conclusion that negative feelings drain our energy, and they are toxic to our work environment and our personal lives, as well as literally chemically toxic to your brain. Positive feelings, on the contrary, are extremely powerful and very much conducive to productivity and to producing high-quality results.

We will cover emotional intelligence and means to improve it, in order to sustain this pillar.

3. Mind:

This pillar refers to how we use our energy. You could be extremely energized, and feel positive emotions, but distractions and lack of focus will make you spend your energy, the same way a dog spends his while chasing his tail. Most of the practices that will help you achieve proper focus are the ones we covered during Time Management: Having clear MITs for the day, single-tasking, working in batches and prioritizing.

There's one extra element that we will discuss in this chapter: meditation.

4. Spirit:

This pillar refers to how we can draw energy from the things that give our life a sense of meaning and purpose. This purpose is the source of the transcending part of our lives, what makes us feel accomplished when looking back from our last day alive.

We can surely find purpose in our work. For example, I've made my career in Oil and Gas, a very controversial industry; but that's not how I see it. We live in a world that runs on energy and uses polymers derived from oil in the tiniest of things. My work helped contribute to attending the needs of billions of people. If you really think about the way your work impacts your life and others', you'll find lots of purpose.

Family, friends and volunteer causes are also excellent sources of Spiritual Energy. In general, living a life full of compassion for others and for yourself, helps you renew your spiritual energy. In a book by Steven Pinker called "The Better Angels of Our Nature: Why Violence Has Declined", he mentions a fairly direct and non-religious source of spiritual wisdom: reading books that tell stories about the hopes, fears, passions and drives of people in distant times in history and faraway regions in the world. That develops the sense of compassion and wisdom. Besides from this, we won't have any specific sections on techniques for this particular pillar because it is very personal to each of us, but there is an overlap between the techniques that apply to Emotion and Mind that will also help you nourish spiritual energy. P.S.: Religion can be a source too.

Breathing

"Winning is the most important thing in my life, after breathing.
Breathing first, winning next."
- George Steinbrenner

In eastern culture, Qi (a.k.a 氣, chi or ki), is life's energy, and it flows through our bodies. Oxygen acts in a similar manner, it comes into our body, passes through our lungs, oxygenates our blood and flows through our whole body, keeping us alive from the cells up. Breathing keeps us alive. But breathing well keeps us well, as well.

Extending your exhalation:

The best way to breathe is by constantly renewing all the oxygen in our lungs. In our modern agitated life, we tend to inhale too shallow, filling our lungs only up to the chest area. By doing so, we leave "old" air in the bottom of our lungs. This stale air occupies space and prevents us from getting larger quantities of "new" air, richer in oxygen. To fully replenish your lungs with fresh air, you must learn to extend your exhalation, letting all the old air out.

Exercise # 1
1. Inhale normally
2. Open your mouth and exhale, until you feel there's completely no air left inside you.
3. At this point close your mouth and let the air come in through your nose; let it be natural, don't try to control your air intake.
4. Repeat this exercise several times while you enjoy doing so. You might get a bit dizzy due to the larger amount of oxygen intake, and if you do so, take a little break, or exhale a bit slower.

This exercise is reinvigorating. You can use it whenever you're feeling shortness of breath after physical activity, or when experiencing anxiety. Another way you can learn how to extend your exhalations is by increasing the duration of your exhales one second at a time.

Exercise # 2

1. Breathe in for two seconds
2. Breathe out for two seconds
3. Breathe in for two seconds
4. Breathe out for three seconds
5. Keep the inhale time constant and increase the exhale time, one second at a time, until you reach five seconds.

Do this exercise for 1 minute. This is an exercise in mindful breathing, so as we concentrate on our breathing, we let our mind relax from other wandering thoughts, and this ultimately helps increase our focus after completed. We'll come back to this when we tackle meditation later in this section.

Belly breathing:

Belly breathing, a.k.a diaphragm breathing, is how we naturally breathe as children. This technique is the most efficient way of regulating our body; it can help you decrease your heart rate, control your sexual energy, recover from exhausting activities, etc. It does wonders, but as adults we rarely breathe this way. Shallow breathing becomes a habit. I partly blame the flat belly canon of beauty, as belly breathing inflates it, so we probably unconsciously acquire the habit of hiding our excess by breathing down no further than our chests. To modify our breathing habits, we need to train our body and our brain.

Exercise # 3

1. While wearing light clothes, or no clothes, lay down on your back and place your palms on your belly, bellow the navel.
2. Breathe slowly in and out through your nose. As you breathe in, feel the air fill your lungs. Your hands will feel how your belly starts rising. Your shoulders might already be used to the tension caused by breathing with your chest, so remember to relax them.
3. When you feel comfortable breathing deeply, try pushing the air out by contracting your stomach, as if your hands were pushing, but without the actual hand push.
4. Repeat for a few minutes, and stop if you start building up tension.

After the first couple of times, you can start doing this exercise while sitting or standing, as long as you keep a good posture. This exercise needs to be repeated several times a day, for a couple of weeks.

As it becomes easier to expel the air out, start moving your hand towards your crotch. If you don't feel comfortable with this, move them toward your groin. If this is not comfortable enough yet, just move them towards your inguinal area. That should eliminate any discomfort. This progression will help you open your breathing completely. Once you feel you can manage to belly breathe naturally, but still require a conscious effort to do it, then repeat the exercise but breathe out through your mouth, and increase the frequency of your deliberate practice. You can start moving the process to the back of your head by using your hand as a cue, so every time your hand rests on your belly the routine will kick in.

It will probably take you close to one year to form this habit, as it involves modifying a routine that has been repeated millions of times throughout our lives, so it's hard to change it. There are many more breathing techniques out there, most of them coming from Yoga Pranayama. I wouldn't suggest trying any others before mastering the ones we've covered.

Breathing while exercising:

While exercising it's very common to experience a lack of breath, or feeling light headed. This discomfort can be overcome by properly breathing while exercising, something we tend to forget as we are tensing our muscles.

The proper way to do it is:
1. Breathe in on the "descending" part of the exercises
2. Breathe out on the "lifting" part of it.

Avoid holding your breath for a prolonged time as this will reduce blood flow to your brain and heart, and might pose a health risk, especially sensitive with age and high blood pressure.

You'll find that breathing is one of those things you were taught as a child, but never really paid attention to. Remember your teacher asking you to breathe and count to ten whenever she saw you were getting angry, or too emotional? Breathing will help you in more ways than you can imagine, it is also one of the key elements in tantric sex, so take note!

And now, we'll move to our next section: Eating. Like breathing, eating is one of the body's basic needs, but also one we neglect sometimes.

Eating

"Food is your body's fuel. Without fuel, your body wants to shut down."

- Ken Hill

Energy is physically stored in our bodies in the form of sugar (in the blood), protein (in the muscles) and fat (as adipose tissue). What we eat plays a big role in how our body is fueled.

There are countless opinions on how, what, and when to eat. Truth be told, all bodies and metabolisms are different, and there's no single diet to fit all purposes. Reducing body fat, increasing muscle mass and being healthy are the most common objectives that people target with diets. Food should be used to boost your own body objectives, such as the ones I just mentioned. But more importantly, food should be something that we enjoy and that helps us feel energized and fresh.

I've tried many different diets, with different purposes. While growing up, I did a high-protein, low-starch, and low-sugar diet because I was too short... and still am. I also tried fat and carb loaded diets as a teenager because I was too skinny. A decade later I gained a lot of weight and did a zero sugar and zero carbs diet over three months to lose almost 20 lbs (basically Keto's LCHF). And finally, I undertook a caloric deficient diet of only 500 kcal per day, over a month, to lose another 10 lb.

All of those suck big time, and I really don't want to diet like that for a very long time. I've discovered, as many already know, that a balanced diet is much more enjoyable and sustainable. I do cut a lot of food out from my regular eating, but I binge once a week to indulge myself. By indulging I don't mean gluttony.

According to the new revised 2015-2020 Dietary Guidelines for Americans from the USDA, you should eat mostly unprocessed, natural, fresh foods that humans are designed biologically to eat, like protein, vegetables, nuts, and fat, and you should avoid everything else like poison. There are many new scientific findings about what is the best diet (with new findings coming out all the time), and there is no one size fits all solution, but there are some basic principles.

My go-to rules are pretty simple:

1. **Eat slowly and chew properly without overeating**: This is key! The brain takes up to 20 minutes after you're full to acknowledge it. If you eat too fast, you can easily over eat. Plus, eating slowly comes with chewing more, and this lubricates the food better and makes it easier for your body to digest and extract the nutrients in your meal.

2. **Consume ONLY complex carbohydrates:** Potato, brown rice, whole wheat bread and pasta, corn. And avoid all processed chips, white bread, regular pasta, processed noodles, cakes, pies, etc.

3. **Always eat vegetables:** To make it easier for myself, I always make the same salad consisting of lettuce, kale (or chard), rocket, tomato, black olives and avocado, and seasoned with olive oil, a pinch of salt and lemon. All commercial salad dressings are forbidden.

4. **No beverages with food:** I drink plenty of water throughout the day, but not with foods. And after finishing my meals I enjoy having tea or coffee depending on the time of day.

5. **No added sugar, not even honey:** Pretty self-explanatory. This rule means no treats with added sugar.

6. **Choose oil accordingly:** I use coconut oil instead of butter (for most recipes), avocado oil to sauté and cook, olive and sesame oil to season and peanut oil in the rare case I need to fry something.

7. **All meals need to have some form of protein, and must never consist of carbs only:** So regardless of the snack, it must contain vegetarian protein like nuts, beans, lentils, chickpeas, etc. or animal protein like eggs, fish, turkey, chicken, beef, cheese, bacon, etc. It is not recommended to eat red meat more than three times a week as it increases cardiovascular risk. I've been a vegetarian since December 2015 and haven't look back.

8. **Whenever possible choose home made over processed or restaurant-served:** Labels, menus, and waiters can claim whatever they want, but you're only 100% certain of what's in your dish when you make it yourself.

9. **Tea and coffee:** All the tea I want up till 6 pm, after that only herbal tea. And coffee up to 6 cups per day and never after 6 pm. By Colombian standards, a coffee cup is half a mug.

10. **Drink 1 gallon of water per day:** Remember the example I gave at the beginning regarding water consumption? Well, I do it. Two liters in the morning and two in the evening. Water comes from all sources, including food, so the gallon is not strictly drunk.

11. **Avoid foods that have more than 5 ingredients on their labels:** This is an indication of how processed the food is.

12. **One binge day:** For me it's Saturday, and it usually means having a traditional Colombian breakfast, some fast food for lunch, and popcorn for movies. I still stick to my #1 rule, so I never overeat during my binge day. Sometimes I go for a binge meal instead of a full binge day.

I go by this rule with a Pareto approach. If I can't eat at home, or go to try out a new restaurant, or even when having a meal at a friend's house: sticking to most of my rules is enough to give me peace of mind. It is ok to bend the rules about once a month, as long as it doesn't become a habit.

Note on the beverage rule:
For some reason, the craziest part of my rules is not drinking any beverages while eating. Some people are shocked by this. I guess they can't imagine themselves not choking on their food if they don't drink something to gulp down their bites. I think people eat too fast and half-chew their food, so they can't physically swallow what's in their mouths. The solutions to avoiding this choking hazard are extremely easy: take smaller bites and chew more. Having any object in the mouth stimulates saliva production, biologically designed to help you swallow your food. You can try it out when brushing your teeth: keep your toothbrush for a minute inside your mouth and you'll find yourself drooling all over!

Other than the beverage, most people I've recommended it to agree that this diet is balanced, easy to follow, sustainable and healthy. Eating like this ensures having enough energy for basal metabolic consumption so that you won't feel sluggish or lethargic. And you'll have enough fat and protein to keep your brain sharp and focused.

Note on Protein sources:
I've decided to make vegetables my main source of protein. I've cut back on milk products (including cheese and natural yogurt) and flesh (from cow, pig, birds and fish). So far I have experienced a good amount of energy, mental sharpness, and good mood. I've also lost over 10 pounds of fat, maintained my muscle weight and exercise regularly.

The important thing is having a good amount of protein, regardless of the source you're using, preferably if it's unprocessed and makes you feel good and energized after you've finished eating it.

Note on medical conditions:
Before undertaking any changes in the way you eat, it is important to consult with your physician first. There are specific requirements for specific diseases. Some examples could be: increased intake of salt for hypothyroidism or hypotension, decreased carbohydrates for diabetics (including complex carbohydrates), decreased salt for hypertensive people, etc.

Note on eating protocols:
I've completely adopted intermittent fasting (IF); both 16/8 and OMAD protocols. These are: eating for a window of 8 hours per day while fasting the other 16, o eating only One Meal A Day, and have found them extremely powerful and in-line with becoming more productive, specially OMAD. I break the protocol on weekends and special occasions.

With better breathing and eating habits, you will feel better and more determined to exercise. In the next section, I'll go through a particular approach that can be adopted by most people.

Exercising

> *"Reading is to the mind what exercise is to the body."*
> - Joseph Addison

As you may already know, exercise has many positive effects on your life: it helps you relieve stress, get better sleep, sharpen focus, live longer, boost your metabolism and immune system, etc. All of these benefits help you become more productive, but I want to discuss exercise mainly from the energy point of view. A study involving 6800 people concluded that 90% of people who exercised regularly reported an improvement on their fatigue levels. This improvement could be explained by another study that showed that exercise improves the mitochondrial content that generates power to meet the body's energy requirements. Exercising helps your body produce energy, making you feel better and less tired, which might seem counterintuitive.

Although there are many different ways to exercise, there is one particular way that will help you achieve better results at raising you mitochondrial content and boost your energy: High-Intensity Circuit Training (HICT) or High-Intensity Interval Training (HIIT). A study published in The Journal of Physiology in 2008 by Kirsten A. Burgomaster, Krista R. Howarth, *et al.*, concluded that:

> *"Given the markedly lower training volume in the SIT (sprint interval training) group, these data suggest that high-intensity interval training is a time-efficient strategy to increase skeletal muscle oxidative capacity and induce specific metabolic adaptations during exercise that are comparable to traditional ET (endurance training)"*

What this means is that short spans of time doing high-intensity exercise can be better for boosting metabolism than long periods of exercise, like running, swimming or riding a bike. This reasoning comes from comparing selected metabolic markers and noting that the high-intensity training for 30 minutes (including rest), three times a week, had very similar results to the one from endurance training of 1.5 hours per training session, three times a week.

There are some great alternatives to exercising this way. Some of these are:

- **HIIT/HICT:** This consists of performing exercise series in sequence, with short rest times in between. The routines can include several types of workouts depending on the desired objectives.
- **Tabatas:** These are exercises performed in an all-out (intensive) manner for 20 seconds, followed by 10 seconds of low intensity. This high-low sequence is repeated eight times, and it's completed over the course of 4 minutes.
- **CrossFit:** This is a training philosophy that combines HIT, weight lifting, and other exercises, where people compete with their training group. It takes 45 minutes per session and it is very intense.
- **Functional Training:** Similar to CrossFit, but without the competing part, this training combines different exercises but focuses on building strength and endurance on the groups of muscles that we use on our day to day routines, generally letting the muscles act against the body's own weight, instead of iron weights. It usually takes 45 minutes as well.

In my opinion and experience, HIIT/HICT is the best place to start building strength and endurance. I have fibromyalgia, and that means I have pain all over my body. This condition makes it difficult for me to exercise, but ironically, being stronger helps reduce the pain. On top of this, I have a shoulder injury, and it is very easy for me to get a new injury under these circumstances. That's why I designed a training program that I could use for myself to be able to build enough strength to allow me to choose any training modality I wanted. I turned this into an App called Six Weeks to Fit (6w2 Fit). The app uses HICT and progressive overload to help the user reach some impressive strength and fitness goals. If you want to improve your strength, I would recommend you to try my app or one of the alternatives.

In my case, I used my app until I felt I was strong enough to avoid getting injured. And then I decided to use a program called Freeletics that also combines HICT and progressive overload, but uses more advanced movements, and is a lot more demanding. I went for this particular program because it is community-based, so you can get some support. I can do it at home and with very little or no special equipment, and due to the nature of the exercises, I have more control and avoid getting injured. Also, I occasionally do Tabatas. The protocol is easy to follow, plus there are lots of free apps to help you do it. This routine is very demanding to perform, but it it is a great way to build endurance. CrossFit is a better match for very athletic and competitive people: not my objectives. Plus, this modality has a high chance of injuries.

Functional Training is an excellent alternative. This one can be done solo, with the aid of apps, or with a gym membership and trainers and group support, like CrossFit, so, since I'm trying to be lean on time and resources, this last option was ruled out. The best option for functional training is to use bodyweight exercises (movements whose force oppose the weight of the body, like situps or pushups), also light on equipment (basically, you would need just a chair and a wall), and it can be done in tabata style.

A very good option is the seven-minute workout. It's based on 30 seconds of repetitions for each exercise, spaced by 10 seconds of rest between exercises. The exercises are: jumping jacks, wall sit, push-ups, abdominal crunch, step-up onto a chair, squats, triceps dip on a chair, plank, high knees running in place, lunge, push-up and rotation, and side plank. There are several YouTube videos and apps for different device platforms that can guide you in the correct form and movement of each exercise, as well as the timing, for a complete and wholesome seven-minute workout. The downside of this workout is that it doesn't lead to muscle growth or fat burning, it should be treated as a maintenance routine, or a minimum effort. If you want to grow muscle and burn fat using this, it's better to do it at least twice every day, instead of once per session, three times per week.

You can choose how you want to exercise. I base my suggestions in getting good results quickly, to help you stay motivated, but my suggestions are by no means the only way to get energized and stay healthy. Schedule an appointment with your medical doctor and discuss what could work better for your needs. Your health must be your priority. I hope this moves you to start working out if you don't already. Try to review the section on creating new habits, and be patient and persistent. This habit is probably the one with the biggest impact that you can create for yourself.

But it can't all be work all the time! Since we also need to sleep and rest, and because it plays such an important role in how much energy we'll have throughout our days, we'll discuss further on sleeping in the next section.

Sleeping

"There is a time for many words, and there is also a time for sleep."
- Homer

Although we all know that sleeping helps us recover, most of us start stealing time from our sleeping time to catch-up on things we claim to not have time do otherwise. That's a big mistake.

When I was in college, I used to feel guilty if I slept too much, like I was wasting my productive time. After that I got a job that was very extreme with the working hours, and staying awake for extended periods of time was expected and regular. I've been "awake" for periods longer than 48 hours, and the physical and mental toll is steep. Also, having to switch between day and night shifts was very common. I learned to appreciate sleep after being deprived of it; it wasn't optional. I started to read up on sleeping, and quickly learned about all the benefits from a good sleep, at the right time.

Some of the benefits:
1. Improved memory: A study that analyzed differences between a group sleeping 6.5 hours and another sleeping 7.5 hours revealed that the group that slept longer had 40% better memories compared to their counterparts.
2. Improved immune system: Research has found a correlation between several markers linked to immune system improving with better sleep.
3. You get more energy: During the Deep Sleep phase, a.k.a restorative sleep, our bodies recover, and our minds consolidate memories. Our body releases hormones and gets oxygenated, and our tissues recover.

4. Your brain cleans toxins during your sleep.

Other benefits include improved focus and reaction time, which can help prevent accidents, especially while driving, improved blood pressure and blood sugar levels, improved mood stability, improved learning ability for both mental and physical skills, and it helps against depression. These are all pretty straightforward reasons to care about getting a proper sleep.

Our sleep cycles have mostly fixed durations. They are not accurate-to-the-minute, but we could say that overall the cycles take around 90 minutes. This lapse is the reason behind the 7.5 or 9 hours sleep periods. In reality, the best approach is to wake up when we are in light sleep. Many apps have a "smart alarm" functionality, which monitors our sleep (using audio and movement sensors) to establish the best moment to sound the alarm. This smart trigger allows you to wake up not feeling groggy or disoriented.

In his informative and entertaining book about the science of sleep, the dangers of sleep disorders, and the power of lucid dreaming, "Night School: Wake up to the Power of Sleep", Richard Wiseman talks about a sleeping-hack called the ninety-minute rule.

> *"You will feel most refreshed when you awake at the end of a ninety-minute sleep cycle because you will be closest to your normal waking state. To maximize the chances of this happening, figure out when you want to wake up, then count back in ninety-minute blocks to find a time near to when you want to go to sleep.*
>
> *Let's imagine that you want to wake at 8 a.m., and wish to go to sleep around midnight. Chunking back in ninety-minute segments from 8 a.m. would look like this:*
> *8 a.m. – 6:30 a.m. – 5 a.m. – 3:30 a.m. – 2 a.m. – 12:30*

a.m. – 11 p.m.

In this example, you should fall asleep around either 11 p.m. or 12:30 a.m. in order to feel especially refreshed in the morning."

So, regarding duration, I would suggest planning for 8-9 hours of sleep and set a 30 minute "listening time" (the window of time where it would trigger the alarm if you are in light sleep) for the sleep monitoring gadget to wake you.

Sleeping Hacks:
Now, let's dig a little bit into other sleeping hacks that will help you manage your sleep better.

1. **Sleep in a dark environment:** Light suppresses the production of melatonin, which is one of the ways our body and brain know it's time to sleep. If you have appliances with led lights, a tiny piece of electrical tape can make them go away.

2. **Avoid blue light:** All screens have this type of light, which makes our brain think it is daytime, causing the same melatonin suppression effect mentioned before. Limit your screen time before bedtime.

   Other means of improving on this point is adjusting the warmth of the light from the screens. You can do this with a software called F.Lux on your computer (MAC or PC), which dims the blue light according to sunset/sunrise times on your geographic location. There are also apps for smartphones (I use one called Twilight on my Android devices) with the same functionality. The caution with this hack is that since it changes the contrast and warmth of the light, color is affected, so if you need to work on color-sensitive projects perhaps you should turn these applications off.

3. **Avoid big meals before sleeping:** If you don't, you might suffer from a. Acid reflux, b. Nightmares or c. Insomnia.

4. **Avoid caffeine and other stimulants in the evening:** I stop 4 hours before my ideal bedtime (10 pm), but some people recommend stopping much earlier, around 2 pm. It depends on how quickly you metabolize the drink.

5. **Avoid alcohol:** Nightcaps, contrary to popular belief, don't help you sleep better. While it might make you feel drowsy and fall asleep faster, it induces dual brain activity patterns between delta and alpha waves, which is not a regular pattern, and it ultimately reduces the quality of your sleep.

6. **Remove notifications and electric hums:** Unless you're expecting a call or your partner or kids are out of the house, put your phone in silence and remove vibrating notifications as well. Also, you can make your room quieter by disconnecting all the appliances that you don't use during the night (TV, lamps, DVD, Blu-ray, decoders, etc.), as they produce a humming noise caused by the transformers used to convert AC current (from the outlet) into DC current (used by devices.)

7. **Mind the plants in your room:** Most plants produce CO_2 during the night, so if you have a significant amount of them is not exactly healthy to have them where you sleep. There are other plants, like the Snake plant, that actually release oxygen at

night and are recommended by some as good bedroom additions.

8. **Choose the right sleeping position:** Depending on different factors like breathing problems, specific body pain, etc. your sleeping position can help you improve your sleep. You can find a very broad guide in the article from the Wall Street Journal listed under the Bibliography & Additional References.

9. **Set an alarm to hit the sack:** When we are at home, and at night, natural occurring cues are difficult, so set an alarm to induce your healthy sleeping habit of going to bed at the same time, every day. This will help you get your needed 8-9 hours of sleep consistently.

10. **Stop using snooze for wake up alarms:** Remember how I told you before that I had periods of time when waking up was difficult? This might happen for several reasons, like depression, being actively disengaged with your job, accumulated fatigue, among other things. In all cases, the alarm snooze option works against us; you snooze, you lose! It keeps us in a restless stage of self-loathing that makes us miserable. It's just too easy to press it until waking up is inevitable, but we don't get up as energized. If you start using the smart alarm option or the ninety-minute rule, as mentioned before, plus you start avoiding snooze, you can start getting up more easily.

11. **Recount the MITs you wrote the night before:** As soon as you wake up, give that day instant purpose by recalling those Most-Important-Things that will make your day.

These are the same hacks I used to get my sleeping hygiene in check after neglecting it for so long. That feeling of waking up full of purpose and energized has a great impact on all other aspects of our life, and your work will quickly reflect it.

In the end, the time we take away from our sleep is added to our sleep debt. Unfortunately, you can't oversleep to have a positive balance on you sleep debt. Too much sleep has the same bad effects on health and cognition as too little sleep, so try your best to make your sleeping pattern consistent, even on the weekends. We'll now move to the section that will help us manage our energy from the second energy pillar, dealing with a very important aspect of cognition: emotion.

Emotional Intelligence

> *"I think for leadership positions, emotional intelligence is more important than cognitive intelligence. People with emotional intelligence usually have a lot of cognitive intelligence, but that's not always true the other way around."*
> - John Mackey

> "Life is 10% what happens to you and 90% how you react to it."
> - Charles R. Swindoll.

There's a theory that proposes that there are nine types of intelligence: Musical–rhythmic and harmonic, Visual–spatial, Verbal–linguistic, Logical–mathematical, Bodily–kinesthetic, Interpersonal, Intrapersonal, Naturalistic, and Existential. If we link Intrapersonal and Interpersonal we get a more sophisticated type of intelligence known as Emotional Intelligence (EQ).

Emotional Intelligence is Batman's unrecognized super power: The ability to manage your emotions rationally, from an objective point of view, and for the common good. Think of it as empathy. It allows you to acknowledge your emotions and those of others and work through them to react accordingly. This theory has been attributed to several authors, but it became widely-known in 1995 with Daniel Goleman and the publication of his book, "Emotional Intelligence: Why It Can Matter More Than IQ".

This concept has been taken in several contexts: schools, parenting, relationships, business, etc. And like any other intelligence, it is one you can improve. In the book "Emotional Intelligence 2.0" by Travis Bradberry and Jean Greaves, emotional intelligence is divided into the following:

- **Self-awareness:** Recognizing how you are feeling.
- **Self-management:** Deciding the best way to react to your emotions.
- **Social awareness:** Recognizing how others are feeling. This one has a lot to do with empathy.
- **Relationship management:** Treating other people with consideration for their emotions.

You've probably heard the quote by Swindoll about the importance of your reactions in life. Emotional intelligence allows you to react in a positive manner. By working on your EQ, you will understand that you have a lot of control over your life, and by taking responsibility for that control you can see any event through a more positive perspective, one that you can deal with. You can turn situations that might otherwise seem negative into positive ones, and this power allows you to control your emotional pillar. You can become more productive by avoiding energy depletion caused by negativity.

This subject is very interesting, so I highly recommend you to read the book "Emotional Intelligence 2.0." You can achieve a balanced emotional life, peaceful and contemplative. In such a state, you can develop the third energy pillar, the mind. That's the subject of the next section.

Meditation

Meditation has gained a lot of buzz over the last decade, and for good reason: it helps you live a more peaceful and productive life. Reading about meditation is very inspiring, it sounds like something so spectacular that you can't understand why it's not part of your life already, and then you try it, and get frustrated very quickly. This frustration is most likely coming from some misconceptions we have about this practice. It might seem too spiritual and you don't have any of those beliefs, or it may seem like a waste of time, it is impossible for you to clear your mind, you can't find the time to do it, etc. I can relate to probably all of the above. But I kept reading about the wonders of meditation, and how it helps increase focus and reduce stress, things that could help me manage my Mind and Spirit pillars better, so I decided to take little steps towards it.

From my research, I found out that there are different ways and techniques to meditate, some requiring more commitment and work than others. I chose the one portrayed as the easiest and shortest: Mindful meditation, which is mostly mindful breathing; this means concentrating on your breathing, feeling the air fill your lungs, raise your chest and belly, etc. So your mind is not truly empty, you are focused on your breathing. But this doesn't last long, pretty quickly your mind starts to wander to pending tasks, new ideas, shopping lists, etc. And this is where meditation starts building our capacity to focus: you need to learn to acknowledge those rushing thoughts and then let them go. By doing so, you consciously tell your subconscious that it is ok not to react to any of those things at that moment, and focus only on your breathing.

To help myself accomplish that, I started using a free app called: Stop, Breathe and Think (SBT). The brilliant thing about it is that the sessions are super short (from 5 to 15 minutes), and they have an algorithm to help you choose a package according to your state of being (physically and mentally). There are other options, I've tried a few, but SBT is still my preferred one among both free and paid apps. This preference is probably very particular for everyone, so try at least three different apps before committing to one. Headspace and Calm are also popular. If you want to take a different approach that doesn't involve apps or technology, you can practice mindful walking: choose a route that is not crowded, and hopefully not noisy, preferably with vegetation (trees or grass), to walk slowly while concentrating on your breathing for 5 to 20 minutes.

You might still be concerned about not having time to meditate, but we've already discussed that it could be as short as 5 minutes, and we've also learned how to create habits. So just link this new behavior to any of your current habits (like meditating right after lunch, or as soon as you wake up, etc.), whatever works best for you. Do keep in mind that the benefits might be instantaneous for some people, but for the vast majority of us mortals, it takes some time before we start feeling the freeing effects of meditation, so be patient and give yourself the chance of experiencing the benefits.

Other Things That Deplete Your Energy, And How To Combat Them

So far, we've learned how we can foster our energy. In this last section of the chapter, we'll review some things that suck away our energy like vampires and we don't even notice. Let's go over some energy depletion mechanisms so we can put it all together before tackling specific things we can do to combat them.

Ego depletion:

Once we have used up our willpower, our capacity to control ourselves is reduced. Making decisions taxes your willpower and ultimately leads you toward ego depletion.

Clutter and Excess:

When you have clutter, physical and digital, your focus is lost as these messy items compete for your attention. Too much stuff is also bad for focus: too many books, too many clothes, too many shoes, and the list goes on. Even if the items are organized they add a spectrum of choices that will probably contribute to ego depletion.

Negative people:

Negativity spreads very easily, even more than positivity. Positivity helps us nourish our creativity, reduces stress, and helps us focus. If you allow negative people to ramble about whatever is bothering them, you'll get your mind boggled by it.

Negative Gossip:

Office gossip not only consumes productive time but also

feeds the poor communication culture of talking behind other people's back. And, since the gossip is supposed to be secret, even seeing the person subject of the rumor makes your mind wander and hypothesize (waste time and energy) on their situations. It also tears down trust amongst working peers, which in turn makes everything much slower.

Avoiding confronting issues:

Most of us tend to avoid conflict by not dealing with the issues at hand. What we don't realize is that problems don't just go away, and by ignoring them, we're just letting them grow in the background, sometimes to a point where they can cause significant damage. Our over-active minds visit those neglected problems from time to time, which makes us enter our procrastination mode.

Busywork:

It is easy to get overburdened with little tasks, to the point where we sometimes end up doing none of the important ones. Most of this busywork comes from other people's priorities, and by accepting it we compromise our own.

Things we can do to fight back:

Don't worry, all is not lost. The logic behind the things we can do to avoid energy depletion is reducing decisions or avoiding them altogether. You can do this by organizing ahead, automating tasks, tidying up your environment, simplifying your life, facing problems, and visualizing your decisions.

1. **Organizing ahead:**

Organizing is dealing with complexity, and life itself is made of complexity all over. To illustrate some highlights of organizing, I'll focus on the field of clothing. We touched on this topic back in the section on ego depletion, but I'll give you a few more pointers. Of course, this doesn't necessarily apply to everybody, you should accommodate to your preference. I'll use three categories.

A. Extreme: Wear only one or two styles, like Steve Jobs.

B. Intermediate: Reduce the amount of clothing in your wardrobe to just 20% (applying Pareto). To do this, put on every piece of clothing you have and while looking in the mirror ask yourself these questions: Do you feel comfortable? Do you like the way you look? Are the fabrics still in good condition? If yes to all keep, if not, discard.

Once you get rid of the obvious candidates, hang your clothes again but with the hanger facing you (inverted to how you usually hang them). You will evaluate if you wear all your things, so after three months you'll be able to see what you don't wear by looking at the hangers, if still inverted: discard.

C. Basic: Whether you choose just to keep one style, or reduce your wardrobe, that's up to you. The basic thing you should do is this: prepare what you'll wear in advance.

Choosing what you'll wear the night before is the easiest. Another way, and how I do it, is creating a rotation method.

I noticed I buy my shirts in the same five colors, but different designs. So I decided to hang them one by one in color sequence, for example blue, gray, brown, red, and others (minorities). And then repeating the pattern. I pick the shirt I wear from the left side of the closet, taking the one hanging leftmost. As I wear and wash my shirts, I hang the newly washed on the right side of the closet. This rotation ensures I never have to choose the shirt I wear, I won't wear a similar shirt two days in the same week, and I won't wear the same shirt for at least 25 days.

For pants, I just have four pairs of pants that can be easily combined with those shirt colors, I grab the pants that correspond to the shirt's color. But in any case, black pants and blue jeans go well with all. For folded clothing, like underwear, I do the cycle as well, and I also stack them in three dominant colors, allowing me to choose according to shirt color. I only break this for special occasions that require more formal or informal wear. Also for traveling where the weather will factor in. This system works pretty well for me, but my wife scoffs at the idea of doing this for herself. So, every day she complains "I don't know what to wear, I don't have enough clothes!" And she has three full closets. She should read this book, and stop calling me a neat freak.

2. Automating (bills, alarms):

There are lots of things we can automate in our lives thanks to technology. Bills are a good example. For all the ones that you can set as automated electronic payments, do it. This automation will remove some stress and save you time. It's easy to set alarms for this on your smartphone, use them to help you with your habit building, for waking up better, to remind you to leave work on time, etc. They serve as pseudo cues.

3. Tidying up and schedule maintenance:

Having a tidy workspace will do wonders for you, you'll find it easier to focus on the important things. This also extends to your house, so keeping things tidy and uncluttered is crucial. For this purpose, I recommend the book *"The Life-Changing Magic of Tidying Up: The Japanese Art of Decluttering and Organizing"* by Marie Kondo. You can also read the article from Farnam Street referenced in the Bibliography & Additional References before doing so, to get an idea of what the book is about.

You can schedule maintenance tasks, like doing the laundry, changing the sheets and towels, or cleaning floors, on a weekly and monthly schedule. But you should stick to it! For real! By setting these parameters, you stop worrying about when you should do this or that. I take the whole Sunday for this, so it doesn't get in the way of my work during the week, or my party and relaxing time during Friday night and Saturday.

4. Simplify

Let me use the following quotes to illustrate how simplifying your life can help you nourish your energy and happiness:

> *"The richest man is not he who has the most, but he who needs the least."*
> - Anonymous

> *"...If you don't have many possessions then you don't need to work all your life like a slave to sustain them, and therefore you have more time for yourself."*
> - Jose Mujica.

Be pragmatic about the things you own, keep what you do use and what makes you feel good. For example, if you keep a book that you always mean to read, but never actually get around to reading, you will stress every time you see it, as it makes you feel like you are short of time or don't have enough commitment. You will feel a lot better if you re-purpose that book as a gift for someone who will use it, or donate it to a library. This will not only take your burden away, but it will also help someone else. The simpler you make your life, the better. Steer clear of filling your life with objects and things, fill it with experiences and people instead. Apply this simplifying strategy to people that bring negativity to your life: remove them as quickly as they appear, don't let their darks roots settle around you.

5. Confront problems:

Running away from problems is easy, but nothing good in life comes easy. If you do face a problem, breathe, use your emotional intelligence, acknowledge how the problem makes you feel and move past it. Deal with problems with people when they occur, letting the moments pass will make dealing with them awkward later; it might even seem resentful if you bring issues at later times. Remind your counterpart that your main interest is getting over the issue, and that it doesn't need to get personal. Make it known what is there to gain if the situation is resolved.

6. Use mental models to take better decisions:

Models are representations of behaviors, and since we live in a complex world, there's no one model to model them all (LOTR pun intended). Instead, we have a toolbox full of simple models ready for use.

Covering this falls outside the scope of this course, but let me point you in the right direction. Take the Coursera free course called Model Thinking from the University of Michigan, designed and taught by Scott Page. This course will help you make better decisions and understand some of our society's dynamics. It's fascinating and applicable to all fields of work and knowledge. Aside from that course and the books Scott mentions, I would also add the book: *"Predictably Irrational: The Hidden Forces That Shape Our Decisions"* by Dan Ariely. In this book you will learn how some of our irrational behaviors take place, thus allowing you to avoid falling into traps designed to make us decide poorly.

And with this, we finish the chapter on energy management! It's a little energy-demanding to get your mind around all its complex aspects, but it makes up for a good investment in energy savings and returns. In the next chapter, we'll go through communication management, where you'll learn some actionable techniques to improve the way you interact with others.

In a Blink

Let's review the main ideas of this chapter in a blink.

The Pillars

Managing one's energy is probably the most important part of becoming super productive, it will allow you to live a better, more enjoyable life as well. There are four energy pillars, and these are:

1. Body: it refers to our basic needs: the physical ones. It can be boiled down to breathing, eating, sleeping, and body movement,
2. Emotion: it refers to the polarity of your energy: positive or negative.
3. Mind: it refers to how we use our energy.
4. Spirit: it refers to how we can draw energy from the things that give our life sense of meaning and purpose.

Breathing

The first step towards a better breathing is **Extending your exhalation**. This allows fresh air, filled with oxygen, into our lungs. There are two simple exercises to help you:

Exercise # 1
1. Inhale normally
2. Exhale through your mouth until you feel there's completely no air left in you.
3. Close your mouth and let air come in from your nose.
4. Repeat this exercise while you feel good, stop if you start feeling dizzy or discomfort.

Exercise # 2

1. Breathe in for two seconds
2. Breathe out for two seconds
3. Breathe in for two seconds
4. Breathe out for three seconds
5. Keep the inhale time constant and increase the exhale time until you reach five seconds.
6. Do the exercise for 1 minute.

Once you've managed to extend your exhalation, you can learn a new technique: **Belly breathing**.

Exercise # 3

1. With light clothes, or no clothes, lay down on your back and place your palms on your belly, bellow the navel.
2. Breathe slowly in and out through your nose. As you breathe in, feel the air fill your lungs. Your hands will feel how your belly starts rising. Relax your shoulders.
3. When you feel comfortable breathing deeply, try pushing the air out by contracting your stomach, as if your hands were pushing, but without the actual hand push.
4. Repeat for a few minutes, and stop if you start building up tension.

Once it becomes more naturally for you, you can start practicing while sitting and standing. You'll need plenty of practice before you can breathe like this without thinking about it.

Finally, **breathing while exercising** is something we neglect sometimes, ending up with red faces and feeling all dizzy. The proper way to do it:

1. Breathe in on the "descending" part of the exercises
2. Breathe out on the "lifting" part of it.

Doing this will help your body be more energized during exercise, and it will minimize health hazards.

Eating

The rules I follow to stick to a healthy, energizing diet, are:

1. Eat slowly and chew properly without overeating.
2. Consume ONLY complex carbohydrates.
3. For lunch and dinner always eat vegetables.
4. No beverages with food.
5. No added sugar, not even honey.
6. Choose oil accordingly.
7. All meals need to have some form of protein, and must never consist of carbs only.
8. Whenever possible choose home made over processed or restaurant-served.
9. Tea and coffee only up till 6 pm, after that only herbal tea.
10. Drink 1 gallon of water per day.
11. Avoid foods that have more than 5 ingredients on their labels.
12. One binge day while following rule #1.

Exercising

Exercising helps your body produce energy, making you feel better and less tired. Some great ways of exercising are:

- **HIIT/HICT:** exercise series in sequence, with short rest times in between.
- **Tabatas:** exercises performed in an intensive manner for 20 seconds, followed by 10 seconds of

low intensity, completed over the course of 4 minutes.

- **CrossFit:** combines HIT, weight lifting, and other exercises. It takes 45 minutes per session and it is very intense.
- **Functional Training:** Similar to CrossFit, but without the competing part, it usually takes 45 minutes as well.

I recommend conditioning your body with apps like 6w2 fit, and then using an HIIT program like the one from Freeletics, keeping in mind that your health is your main priority.

Sleeping

We all know that sleeping helps us recover, but we still deprive ourselves of it, sometimes for the sake of work. A better strategies is getting a good night sleep that will give you some great benefits, such as:

1. Improved memory.
2. Improved immune system.
3. You get more energy.
4. Your brain cleans toxins during our sleep.

You need 8 to 9 hours of good sleep to get all the benefits.

Sleeping Hacks:

Some sleeping hacks that will help you manage your sleep better are:

1. Sleep in a dark environment.
2. Avoid blue light.
3. Avoid big meals before sleeping.
4. Avoid caffeine and other stimulants in the evening.
5. Avoid alcohol.

6. Remove notifications and electric hums.
7. Mind the plants in your bedroom.
8. Choose the right sleeping position.
9. Set an alarm to hit the sack.
10. Stop using snooze for wake up alarms.
11. Recount the MITs you wrote the night before.

Too little and too much sleep are both bad for you, so try your best to make your sleeping pattern consistent, even in the weekends.

Emotional Intelligence

Emotional intelligence gives you control over your life, and by taking responsibility for that control you can see any event through a more positive perspective. Emotional Intelligence is divided in the following:

- **Self-awareness:** Recognizing how you are feeling.
- **Self-management:** Deciding the best way to react to your emotions.
- **Social Awareness:** Recognizing how others are feeling. This one has a lot to do with empathy.
- **Relationship Management:** Treating other people with consideration for their emotions.

These four elements have traits that you can work on to help you improve your EQ.

Meditation

Meditation helps increase focus and reduce stress. There are different ways and techniques to meditate, the easiest and shortest being: Mindful meditation, which is mostly mindful breathing; this means concentrating on your breathing, feeling the air fill your lungs, raise your chest and belly, etc. while you are focused on your breathing. As you learn how to deal with emerging thoughts, you start building your capacity to focus.

To start meditating, anything from 5 minutes and above count. You can take mindful walks while doing mindful breathing, or you could use apps like Stop, Breathe and Think (SBT), Headspace, or any other form the countless options out in the App Markets.

To truly get the benefits from meditation you to need to practice consistently for some time.

Other things that deplete your energy, and how to combat them

There are things that suck away our energy, and we don't even notice:

- Ego depletion
- Clutter and Excess
- Negative people
- Negative Gossip
- Avoiding confronting issues
- Busywork

Things we can do to fight back:

To fight back this energy-suckers, we need to remove and replace. Some strategies are:

1. Organizing ahead: Simplify your wardrobe, and reduce your decisions.
2. Automating: remove the stress of bills by automating their payments. Use alarms to create cues for habit formation.

3. Tidying up and schedule maintenance: keep a tidy work and home environment. Scheduling maintenance work to takes advantage of batching tasks.
4. Simplify: Keep material things that make good feel good, get rid of the rest. This also applies to people in your life.
5. Confront problems: avoid an unnecessary crisis by dealing with problems as they appear.
6. Use mental models to take better decisions: gear up with frameworks to help you make decisions.

Chapter 6: Communications Management

How This Chapter Came To Be

Having being born in 1983, I still remember when the world was transitioning to emails as the main mean of communication. I didn't see how the workplace was transformed by it, which took place when I was still in high school.

As I was growing up receiving a letter was exciting, and unusual for kids I guess. But at those ages, we had other reasons for communicating, like letting someone know you had a crush on her or thanking someone for the friendship, or in some cases even swearing to become their worst nemesis! Serious stuff that needed to be treated carefully, and we had to do it concisely, as it would probably be folded on top of the same paper it was written in.

Communicating with others is always exciting, and very important, and the world knows it, but even knowing, our education systems neglect to teach us how to communicate effectively with others. Sure, they teach some stuff; I remember I was taught how to write formal letters, its parts, etc… but it was all too impersonal. I had to figure out as I started working what worked and what didn't. It helped me that I ran a Latin American Hip-Hop community online (from 1999 until 2009), and I was always exchanging emails with people from different places, ages, and backgrounds.

When I started working, I was always eager to share

knowledge with my peers, so I built a reputation for coming up with things to make our jobs easier. But I wasn't the only one, most of the people would share experiences and learnings through email. That, on top of a significant amount of emails from clients and management, our inboxes would quickly turn into hundreds of unread emails per day. Very different from the pace of communications I was used to back then. It became evident to me that managing communication would make the difference between being "busy" or "productive." As I grew older, I kept reading about techniques and tips to help me on this front, and the most effective ones are the content of this chapter. Using these I've manages to make zero-inbox a breeze, avoid endless incoming calls to sort out small stuff, and keep my work at work when finishing the workday.

But aside from the productivity perks of communicating well, there are other great benefits, like forging real and long-lasting friendships at work. Earning the respect and support of others by helping them reach their goals. Things that can only be achieved if you're committed to making communication a tool for deepening human interaction.

Communicating With Others

"Wise men speak because they have something to say; fools because
they have to say something."
- Plato

When we communicate effectively, we achieve synergy with our peers and clients. Poor communication slows down progress, damages trust and creates busywork for ourselves and others.

Choosing the Medium of Communication

The first thing we need to do is choose the appropriate medium of communication.

- **For urgent matters:** In-person, call or SMS if you can't get through. **E-mail is not for urgent matters.**
- **If you need a reply throughout the day and/or if there's room for back-and-forth communication:** Instant Messaging using your organization's preferred software (skype, hangouts, etc.)
- **For sensitive matters, or when other means have failed:** Use in-person communication.
- **For matters that need an answer in more than one day:** use e-mail.

When we need to exchange information with peers that work near our station, it is good to establish with them which is the best approach. It might seem easy and efficient just to talk, but remember that this will mean interrupting the other person, and eventually being disturbed yourself. If you are batching tasks, breaks could be a good moment for quick exchanges, but be careful of straying into chit-chat too often.

In any case, regardless of the medium used, always maintain a respectful approach, be cordial, clear and concise. Brevity in words allows carrying the desired message forward, so avoid over complicating things.

Arguing intelligently

When engaging an argument, it is important to keep stay in the pursuit of truth, instead of the pursuit of winning the argument. Real-life interactions are not debates that need to be won. Social interactions are great opportunities to learn new things and share knowledge.

Active listening is a good technique for doing this. As its name suggests, it consists of not only hearing what the interlocutor (your counterpart) is saying, you also need to fully understand the message they are trying to convey. You have to keep yourself from straying from focus, and make sure that you're using non-verbal cues to let it be known that you're paying attention, like keeping direct eye contact, not crossing your arms, nodding, and even with a simple uh-huh every now and again. It is equally important to keep yourself from start thinking of ways to respond, you should first let the other part communicate their full intend before you interrupt them.

To recap:
1. Listen while concentrating and understanding what's being said.
2. Stay focused and avoid letting your mind wander.
3. Use non-verbal cues signal that you're paying attention.
4. Don't interrupt, only speak once the interlocutor has finished, and you have a good grasp of their message.

If there's a conflicting idea, or you need to give a critical commentary, there's some great advice we can take from Daniel Dennett's: In Intuition Pumps and Other Tools for Thinking, it is a short list of rules that he summarized from game theorist Anatol Rapoport:

"How to compose a successful critical commentary:

1. You should attempt to re-express your target's position so clearly, vividly, and fairly that your target says, "Thanks, I wish I'd thought of putting it that way.
2. You should list any points of agreement (especially if they are not matters of general or widespread agreement).
3. You should mention anything you have learned from your target.
4. Only then are you permitted to say so much as a word of rebuttal or criticism."

Following Rapoport's rules will allow a more open and fluid conversation as your counterpart will be more open to your criticisms, or feedback.

Building Relationships

Finally, a study of the American workplaces revealed that strong social connections work in favor of engagement, which in turn works in favor of productivity. So having friends at work is a good way to feel more passionate and happy about work. One of the easiest way to achieve friendship is by finding things in common with your peers, and then exploiting those to build honest and long-lasting friendships. For me, communicating well with others has resulted in creating meaningful friendships with people from all over the world, which by itself is something very empowering, and from a career perspective, is the best way to build a professional network of people that can vouch for your work and human ethics. Nothing speaks louder than social proof, that's why professional networks like LinkedIn are popular and definitive (in some cases) to grow your career.

While you work on growing and sustaining good work relationships, you'll still need to make the most from your communications. In the next section, we'll review how you can get others to respond more effectively.

How To Get People To Respond

"The meaning of a communication is the response it gets."
- NLP Mantra

It is all too easy to send hundreds of emails, and then at some point, you realize that following up all the ones without appropriate responses becomes a job in itself.

So how can we make this better? Well, I would summarize the solution in the following:

1. **Make it personal:** It is usually better to direct your message to one or very few people, instead of cc'ing a complete department.

2. **Answer the five Ws:** What, Who, When, Where & Why; Make sure your subject line is a good summary of **what** the email is about, and elaborate a bit on the purpose of the email in the body of the message. Then state **who** requires taking **what** action, **when** and by **when**. Last, but not least, explain **why** the action is needed. In 1977, a study by psychologist Ellen Langer and her team revealed that people respond 30% more to requests when they are given a reason, even if the reason doesn't make much sense.

3. **Use short phrases and lose the padding:** If your recipients can quickly read and take action on your communication, there is a 42% higher chance that they will. This odds make it important to keep your messages short and straight forward.

4. **Use your signature wisely:** Use your signature to convey information useful to your recipients, like

your contact info and your role in your organization.

5. **Send fewer emails and to fewer people:** when you're interacting with others via email, make sure that you're only including relevant people on the thread. If you avoid copying people needlessly, others will notice that you omitted to add too many parties and will start doing the same when writing their emails.

6. **Use To, CC and BCC wisely:** The convention is to use the **"To"** recipient for the people that need to take action (responsible) and **"CC"** (Carbon Copy) for those who need to be informed. **"BCC"** is a complicated recipient, and it can easily get you into trouble. If the person in BCC receiving that email uses "Reply All", the "To" and "CC" recipients will get the reply and realize that you hid one, or more, extra recipients from them, which might send a mistrusting message; I strongly suggest using BCC only if **all** desired recipients **are under the BCC field**; this way, if any of them hits "Reply All", only you will receive the response.

Even though these tips to improve response are intended for emails, they apply to all kinds of communication. And in the case of face-to-face, I would add choosing the appropriate body language and tone of the conversation. These are the same tips I used to reduce my interactions to get things done more quickly. Although I'll admit that writing short emails is difficult; being concise is way more complicated than just writing whatever pops into your mind, that's why is important to re-read your emails and cut whatever is unnecessary and doesn't add value to the communication.

Sometimes to get a respond you need to sell people your ideas, in the next section you'll learn a couple of ingenious easy ways of doing so.

Writing Style: Copywriting

"Copywriting is written content conveyed through online media and print materials. Copy is content primarily used for the purpose of advertising or marketing. This type of written material is often used to persuade a person or group as well as raise brand awareness."
- Definition from Wikipedia

Copywriting is something we could have covered when we discussed how to get people to respond, but I gave it its own little spotlight here because I think it's important. We want to be able to write our email and communications using copyright to make our messages more appealing and effective.

The first thing you need to know is that people care mainly about themselves. More than they care about you or your needs. Having that in mind, you should always aim to answer the question from your recipients: what's in it for me?

To achieve this I'll cover two common methodologies:
- The ROT formula (borrowed from Neville Medhora)
- The AIDA method

ROT Formula for subjects/headlines

ROT is an acronym that stands for:
R – Results: What they'll get from taking the action you are suggesting.
O – Objections: Attack the reason why they wouldn't take action.
T – Timeframe: How long it would take them to get to the result.

Subjects and Headlines are the very first filter we use to

choose what to read, or what to ignore. If you manage to make good ones, your messages will increase their odds of being opened. The ROT formula is extremely straightforward and easy to use; I'll illustrate this with an example. Say you want to offer a course in negotiation to a client. Said course is one week long, but it is only one hour daily, and it takes place after work hours, the course was designed for introverts and extroverts. Ok, so you have the information, now write each part of the ROT.

Results: learn to negotiate a win-win.
Objection: even if you work fulltime.
Timeframe: in only one week.

You can write different options for each. The more, the merrier. Just mix and read out loud to find the one you like the most. Which of the following sounds better to you?

ROT - Learn to negotiate a win-win, even if you work fulltime, in only one week!
RTO - Learn to negotiate a win-win, in only one week, even if you work fulltime!
ORT - Even if you work fulltime, learn to negotiate a win-win, in only one week!
OTR - Even if you work fulltime, in only one week, learn to negotiate a win-win!
TOR - In only one week, even if you work fulltime, learn to negotiate a win-win!
TRO - In only one week, learn to negotiate a win-win, even if you work fulltime!

It is important to get creative and draft several Results, Objections, and Timeframes.

AIDA:

AIDA is an acronym that stands for:
A – Attention (Awareness): Get the attention of the

recipient, pick their ears up.

I – Interest: Get their interest with interesting facts; use stories, case studies, research, etc.

D – Desire: Show them what their life would be like if they take the action you'll ask from them, the result.

A – Action: Lead them through the process of taking action, make it easy for them to get to it.

If you write your messages using these elements, in this particular order, you're very likely to succeed in getting the recipient's positive response.

Even though these two simple techniques are mostly for marketing and advertisement, keep in mind that most of the time people need to buy into your proposals, so you might as well treat people as potential buyers. It is also a good idea to evaluate if you're writing to customers (even if they are internal), or providers. You shouldn't have to convince providers to provide their services, but if you do, feel free to use these techniques as well.

Managing our outgoing messages is important, but so is managing the incoming ones. In the next section, I will walk you through some actionable techniques to simplify your incoming emails.

Emails: Filter, Prioritize, Archive, Discard

"Email is familiar. It's comfortable. It's easy to use. But it might just be the biggest killer of time and productivity in the office today."
- Ryan Holmes

Ok, so we've discussed when to use emails (replies can wait a day or more), and the etiquette (basic elements an email should contain and how to use the To, CC & BCC fields appropriately). We've also covered the importance of reading your emails in batches (only one or two times a day). Now we'll cover some techniques that can help you go through your email a lot faster.

1. Filter your email:

Filtering emails means organizing your emails in folders. To do so, you need to use a criterion. There are two basic ways of doing this: manually or automatically.

Some people follow the "Getting things done" workflow and create four folders: To-Do, Waiting for a reply, Delegated, and Scheduling (meetings, appointments, etc.) Then, they manually move their incoming emails into those categories. There are many variations to these folders, but either way, this requires a lot of manual work (busywork), so I don't follow, nor recommend this method.

My preferred method is filtering automatically (all email clients have this option), and I use subjects, recipients, senders, domains, etc. To set up rules to automatically sort out all of my incoming emails. By automatically filtering my emails, I can go through them using my priority criteria: First I will read emails coming from my boss and upper management, then scale down. Some categories are bulletins, news, etc. So I don't worry about selecting all emails under those categories and marking them read, to avoid the anxiety of seeing hundreds of unread emails. I do this at the end of my email reading batch, so if I have time, I will do a quick browse to see if something catches my attention. Try to filter in a forward manner, creating one folder for each sender is a lot of work and doesn't add value. Use departments, companies, and other higher level criteria instead.

2. Archive your email:

Remember how we discussed clutter doesn't work in favor of managing your energy? Well, it applies to your digital life as well. Archiving is not deleting, so don't worry about not being able to go back and check a certain email. Archiving is the digital equivalent of taking all the papers from your desk and filing them in drawers for future references. In our digital era, an email that is one month old is very unlikely to have relevance. You can set up your email client to archive emails older than one month from all your folders. If you haven't read them, and your action is still required, you are very likely to receive a reminder from the requester.

I try to reply all the emails addressed to me or that require my input or action, and I can achieve this because I live by Inbox Zero, meaning I normally don't leave unread emails by the end of the day. This method is a bit controversial, but if you follow all the techniques discussed here, you'll find it less haunting.

3. Discard unwanted email:

One of the email rules I never break is: **never use my work email to subscribe to websites, newsletters, courses, etc.** I only use it for work. **I also never send personal emails from my work account**, and if I feel like forwarding an email (e.g. something my company sent regarding family, health or security) to any personal contact,

I first send it to my home email address and then forward it from there.

Because I do this, I seldom receive any spam on my work email. But when I do, I deal with it quickly using two resources: The SPAM filter from my email client and Unroll.me. The latter one is a free service that scans your emails for subscription and automatically filters and marks them as read. After doing that for a full day it gathers all of them and send you one email per day with a summary of all of the "rolled" emails (in my personal email account that's something like 30 emails per day), so you can quickly see snapshots of each and decide if you want to read one or several. If you struggle with deleting emails, like I do, Unroll.me is great because it eases that anxiety, the emails are still in your email account, but they don't scream for your attention with the little number next to the folder, or the bold subject line.

4. Choose the right device:

Reading emails on smartphones or tablets becomes ineffective if the messages need an elaborate response. In these cases, we end up flagging or marking these emails as unread just to re-read them when we get back to our computers, doubling the time of the task unnecessarily. If you start following the batch email reading rule, then you probably get the chance of reading all your emails directly in your laptop, which is ideal. But if, for whatever reason, you end up reading emails on the smartphone, try to use your filter system to sync only important or urgent folders, so you can prioritize the messages you read.

Once you start implementing these techniques, you'll be surprised how easy it is to be extremely effective with email. I've used them to literally manage tenths of thousands of emails: by that I mean: Staying informed of important matters, being responsive to my clients and peers, being respectful to other's people time (by reading and replying to their emails), and kept zero unread emails by the end of each workday (meaning: stop reading emails at home! Remember emails are not for urgent matters).

Sometimes the result you want from a communication is a change in behavior, for example when you are providing feedback. Next section deals with how to provide feedback effectively.

Positive vs. Negative Feedback

"Sweet words are like honey, a little may refresh, but too much gluts the stomach."
- Anne Bradstreet

When we are providing feedback, both praise and criticism are important. There's a study that suggests that the ratio of positive vs. negative feedback directly influences a team's performance.

- **High performers:** Receive 6 positive comments per 1 negative.
- **Mid performers:** Receive 2 positive comments per 1 negative.
- **Low performers:** Receive 1 positive comments per 3 negatives.

If your team doesn't work well, your overall performance will be affected, even if you're highly productive.

The fine art of providing feedback isn't an easy one to master. This doesn't mean that you have to suck miserably at it. Just keep the following key points in mind:

1. **Keep the 6 to 1 ratio in mind:** Recognize the good things other people constantly do and praise them for it.

2. **Be sincere:** There's nothing worse than false praise, it makes you seem hypocritical or sarcastic.

3. **Ask for permission:** If you need to provide negative feedback, prepare the person for it and ask them if they wouldn't mind some feedback.

4. **Don't sugar-coat negative feedback:** Doing so will reduce the importance of it.

5. **Be specific and objective:** Don't ramble and get straight to the point. Be objective about the feedback, and if it's your opinion, make sure you let the other person know that (different to a fact or a group's consensus).

6. **Don't make it personal:** Phrase the feedback in such a way that the person at the other end knows it's not a personal praise, or attack, but a professional courtesy instead.

7. **Choose the right venue:** If you need to provide sensitive feedback, do it privately. If you need to provide feedback on a group's performance, try to get all the members together, but isolated from other non-involved parties.

8. **Keep your emotion in check:** If you have strong feelings about the feedback you're going to provide, be patient and wait until you have your emotional side under control, mind your emotional intelligence.

The key point here is that communicating properly with others can help you a lot, and when it comes to feedback, both positive and negative ones are important in helping others be more successful; just mind the 6:1 ratio. And with this, we've reached the end of the chapter on Communications' Management. We covered why communication matters, some basic rules to choose the appropriate medium to use, some techniques to get a better respond from others, how to manage our outgoing & incoming emails, a couple of writing hacks and finally, why feedback is important and how to provide it.

In the next chapter: Information Management, you will learn how to use information to your advantage, and deal with the increasing media overload. It contains a lot of technology-oriented content, so if you're not very tech savvy it might be ok to skip the last sections, but please go through the first two (Video & Audio and Reading).

In a Blink

Let's review the main ideas of this chapter in a blink.

Communicating with others

If you communicate effectively, you achieve synergy with your peers and clients, and easily increase your productivity. Poor communication does the exact opposite. The first thing you need to do is **choose the appropriate medium of communication**:

- **For urgent matters:** In-person, call or SMS.
- **If you need a reply throughout the day and/or if there's room for back-and-forth communication:** Instant Messaging.
- **For sensitive matters, or when other means have failed:** In-person communication.
- **For matters that need an answer in more than one day:** Use e-mail.

Always maintain a respectful approach, be cordial, clear and concise. Brevity goes a long way.

When engaging an argument, you should aim to **argue intelligently**, doing so allows you to learn new things, and to share knowledge. The best way to do so is by using Active listening that basically consists of listening while concentrating and understanding what's being said while avoiding letting your mind wander. You also have to use non-verbal cues signal that you're paying attention. And finally, don't interrupt; only speak once the interlocutor has finished.

If there's a conflicting idea, you can use Rapoport's Rules: re-express your target's position clearly, list any points of agreement, mention anything you have learned from your target, and only then refute or critic.

Finally, an added benefit of good communication practices is **building relationships** and making friends at work, which a study of the American workplaces revealed works in favor of engagement, productivity, and happiness.

How to get people to respond

To make sure you get the most out of every email you send, follow these guidelines when writing your emails:

1. Make it personal.
2. Answer the five Ws: What, Who, When, Where & Why. Stating why you need a response is key here.
3. Use short phrases and lose the padding.
4. Use your signature wisely.
5. Send fewer emails and to fewer people.
6. Use To, CC and BCC wisely.

Even though these tips to improve response are intended for emails, they apply in all kinds of communications.

Writing Style: Copywriting

Keeping in mind that people care mainly about themselves. More than they care about you or your needs, you can use a couple of Copywriting techniques to sell your ideas and improve your response ratio.

ROT Formula for subjects/headlines

ROT is an acronym that stands for:
R – Results.
O – Objections.
T – Timeframe.

You can try different variations (ROT, RTO, ORT, OTR, TOR, TRO) to find the one that sounds best.

AIDA:

AIDA is an acronym that stands for:
A – Attention (Awareness).
I – Interest.
D – Desire.
A – Action.

This is a time-tested marketing technique to get people to buy in, as it provides value to the recipients before asking to get something in return.

Emails: Filter, Prioritize, Archive, Discard

To help get through your email more effectively, follow these techniques:

1. **Filter your email:** Use automated filtering systems from your email client to organize your emails on high-level folders to help you prioritize urgent and important ones.
2. **Archive your email:** Archive emails that are older than one month to keep your inbox tidy.
3. **Discard unwanted email:** Use SPAM filters and web services like unroll.me to manage unwanted email.
4. **Choose the right device:** Read emails in the device that allows you to answer all required demands. This means reading emails on your computer most of the time.

Used in conjunction with task batching, while single tasking, will help you master Zero-inbox, even if that's not your objective.

Positive vs. Negative Feedback

Providing feedback, both praise and criticism are important. Even though providing feedback isn't an easy thing to do, following key points in mind will help make it easier:

1. **Keep the 6-positives to 1-negative ratio in mind.**
2. **Be sincere.**
3. **Ask for permission.**
4. **Don't sugar-coat negative feedback.**
5. **Be specific and objective.**
6. **Don't make it personal.**
7. **Choose the right venue.**
8. **Keep your emotion in check.**

Communicating properly with others can help you a lot, and when it comes to feedback, both positive and negative ones are important in helping others be more successful.

Chapter 7: Information Management

How This Chapter Came To Be

At some point in life, and being curious about new findings on several topics, I started consuming books, articles, and online courses. I used to spend a lot of time going through a lot of material, but not everything is good all the time. There were plenty of times when I ended up feeling disappointed, with a bad taste in my mouth for having wasted time in uninteresting contents.

After I stumbled upon the Not-to-do List I sought out ways for minimizing the amount of time spent in going through new material, while increasing the quality of my retention. That re-ignited my lost interest in speed Reading, and so I embarked on online courses to learn how to do it. I ended up learning a lot more things about Information Management, and these techniques and skilled came at the right time.

This took place after I quit my field job. I was spending my mornings learning French and then my evenings reading, exercising and doing online courses. When I started my new role in management in a different company, I had tons of document, policies, and technical sheets to go through. Aside from that, the new company has a strong Web Based Training (WBT) culture (as most large corporations do). My recently acquired speeding skills allowed me to catch up quickly and get my certifications done. Not only that, this was also the time I was implementing a lot of new habits to improve my productivity at work, and part of that was expanding my managerial skills, so I started taking courses on MOOCs (Massive Open Online Course) to learn more about project management, corporate finance, accounting, operations' management, etc. And I ended up taking over 25 courses and covering a pseudo-MBA curriculum.

In this chapter you'll learn the techniques I used to achieve productivity in Information Management.

Speed Controls: Video & Audio

"Life is like a ten-speed bicycle. Most of us have gears we never use."
                                                                    - Charles M. Schulz

Two of the most efficient ways to consume information are videos and audio. In our digital era, these two are quite popular via podcasts, YouTube, webcasts, etc.

I've noticed that some are edited and slowed down a little bit as to make it easier for people to understand, and to make contents "longer" than what they originally are. These two reasons might be irrelevant if you are comfortable with the language the information comes in, so you might as well just speed things up!

I love learning new things using online courses (more on this later), so I constantly need to increase the speed of my videos to about 1.5x or 2.0x depending on the media. Some HTML5 players online have the option to do this, but some don't. If you're playing offline media, using the players' options increases the pitch of the voice, making it sound like a chipmunk is talking! Also, making a video slower is wonderful for practicing your listening skills in a foreign language, especially if it also has subtitles.

You can sort this all together using the playback speed controls in Youtube. Although they are a little hidden in the Settings section, under Speed, you can also download browser extensions to make this control easier to use. For example, there is a Chrome extension called 'Youtube Playback Speed Control' that lets you use the up and down arrows (or any custom keys) while watching a video to make it faster or slower. There is also a software called MySpeed. I paid for the pro version to be able to use it offline. And even though it might seem pricey, if you put a dollar value to one of your working hours (your salary divided by the number of hours you're expected to work in a month), then you'll find that the return on investment is quite good and fast. This is especially true if you're doing corporate training and you have to go through several videos during work hours.

This is also how I managed to complete a large number of online courses: My connectivity in Gabon was very limited, so I had to leave the videos downloading during the day in my personal computer, and then going through them after getting home from work. Now that I'm back in my country I can skip the downloading part, and just stream videos while speeding them up. Even if you don't use it for work, leisure and learning with faster media are also good reasons to invest in it. For the offline part, the catch is a limited support of players, you will need to check their website to find out about the options. Of course, not all media is meant to be consumed so fast, don't feel guilty about indulging in some entertainment at 1.0x.

Note: I have no affiliation with this software, the only reason I don't name any alternatives is because I haven't found any.

Power -and Speed- Reading

"Some books are to be tasted, others to be swallowed, and some few to be chewed and digested."
\- Francis Bacon

The way we learn to read in elementary school is a wonderful way to start, but our education systems fail in upgrading the skill as we grow in age and knowledge, which is unfortunate, because even nowadays with the vast amounts of resources found in video and audio, written form is still king. I've done at least four courses about speed reading, and a couple more on power reading. The reason for the redundancy was because I wanted to get as many techniques as I could to learn how to Speed Read. I'll quickly summarize the most important concepts. I strongly suggest reading the post from Shane Parrish found under the Bibliography & Additional References as well.

The following are the main principles of power reading:

1. Choose what to read

The amount of information available to us is exceedingly overwhelming; that doesn't mean that we need to try and read everything we can get our hands on. Sometimes it's easy to choose what to read, and I'll cover these ways of choosing later on when we talk about curated content. But sometimes we end up reading a book or article, only to decide at some point in the middle that it's not what we expected. The Zeigarnik effect states that unfinished tasks continue to creep into our minds. Even if we decide to stop reading, due to the Zeigarnik effect we feel vested with the text and sometimes end up reading it entirely nonetheless.

One skill you can practice in order to avoid investing time and efforts on material that won't add value to you is by systematically skimming through the book. By this, I mean reading the jacket, the back of the book, the preface, studying the table of contents and even going through the book searching for bold or outlined text, graphics, tables, etc. It will give you enough information to determine whether you want to read it or not.

2. Establish how will you read it:

Now that you know whether you will read something, you need to choose how you want to read it. To do this, I use these simple heuristics, according to the type of text:

- **Legal, Health and Instructions:** read in a detailed manner, regardless of the speed.
- **Fiction (novels, stories, etc.):** read in whatever speed I enjoy it the most, usually slow as I like to let my mind wander and recreate what's happening.
- **Articles, emails, non-fiction books and research material:** I try to read as fast as I can (speed-read).

To speed-read, I use the techniques I'll describe next.

3. Expand your visual horizon:

When we learn to read, we first learn the individual sound of the letters and then how they sound when they are joined to another letter, building up to the sound of words. We end up learning to read word-by-word. To increase your reading speed, you must learn to read words grouped together, effectively reading one line of text in 3 or 4 saccades. A saccade is a jolt of eye movement, and the jump can be very small, so that to sweep a line you would use dozens of saccades, or bigger, so that you could jump from one end to the other in one saccade. Sweeping a line of text in 3 to 4 saccades is like dividing a line of text into three or four parts and moving your eyes to the middle of each part, fixating for a very short time. This technique allows you to get the group of words instead of word-by-word. Acquiring this skill takes time and practice, I suggest using a simple and familiar text you have already read to practice.

The number of saccades to use depends a lot on the format of the text; if you have a big computer screen, a line of text may have too many words. The same happens with printed text with small fonts. For computers and digital devices, one easy way to help you read faster is to use *Pocket* to get the text formatted in a read-friendly format. For Kindles and other digital readers, I suggest reading in landscape mode with medium/large sized fonts.

4. **Reduce subvocalization:**

Subvocalization is the term for repeating the sound of the words we read mentally. Some people even move their lips or whisper the words as they read. This unconscious process is a side effect coming from our learning-how-to-read days. If you are using the saccade method to read, you'll naturally decrease your subvocalization, but even then we tend to repeat some of the words, limiting our reading speed to our vocalization velocity.

Another nasty consequence of subvocalization is that we get bored quickly due to our reading speed, and our mind starts to wander while our eyes and body read in auto mode. Or, if we are tired and sleep deprived, we might have a micro-sleep, in which our brain nods off even though our eyes keep open. It's as if the lights are on, but no one is at home. You know this has happened when you reach a point in the text where you can't honestly recall the last paragraphs or pages!

The first thing you need to do is acknowledge how you are doing it, this will give you tools to fight it. You could move your lips, bite a pen or pencil while reading, or try to count from 1 to 3 continuously as you read. The first effect of doing these things is to prove to yourself that you can read and understand even if you're not sub-vocalizing. Once you've acknowledged it and are convinced that you can do without the subvocalization, then you'll have to go through the habit creation cycle and put your willpower to work, and consciously do an effort not to subvocalize.

5. Avoid regressing:

Remember those missing paragraphs or pages? We usually just go back to where we last remember and then re-read. Doing the same thing over and over is highly inefficient, and it becomes a bad habit. But don't fret, there are ways to eliminate this, especially if you have managed to incorporate the points we've already covered. The easiest way and a lot of times the essential technique to speed read is using a pointer to move along the text. You can use a pen, your finger, or a magic wand (for the geeks amongst you) to guide your eyes to your next saccade. This guidance forces your brain to infer that the only way is forward.

If the pointer trick is not enough to keep you from peeking back, another technique is using a piece of paper, or card, or scrolling down, to cover the text above and leaving only new text visible.

6. Pause to recall:

If you recall what we covered in habits to learn better, you'll remember that actively recalling information is one of the things you can do to improve your understanding. Whenever you read a paragraph that you consider has important information you should retain, pause at the end of it and recall the main idea of it. There's no point in reading at the speed of Flash if you won't be able to use that information later on.

7. Choose what to re-read and what to skip:

By re-read, I mean the whole text, and by what to skip I mean just sections of the text. If you encounter a sturdy material that you consider of importance to your life: re-read it at least once. Not because you didn't get it the first time, but because spaced repetitions help you move information into long-term memory.

Now, in some texts, especially the non-fiction ones, there's a lot of padding. I like to think that some authors are aware of the importance of spaced repetitions, and they repeat things they consider important to help you get them better. There's also the fact that regularly people read word-by-word and might wander for a couple of paragraphs without even noticing it, so the author gives the reader the chance of encountering essential information several times in their path. Finally, there's also the chance that the author is adding padding just for the sake of length; as we sometimes are biased by how long a text looks to judge its quality. Even editors and publishers suffer from this. For whatever reason, there's usually repeated material that you can safely skip over. Keep an eye out for it to "read faster".

These points are of course a very rudimentary way of looking at speed and power reading; I wouldn't claim this is all there is to it. But I would say this is enough to get you to read from 200% to 300% times faster than the average reading speed, which, by the way, is 250 words per minute.

With the knowledge you gained from this section and the previous one, you'll be able to make the most out of the following sections, where you'll discover "book summaries", audiobooks and curated content.

Blinkist

"A smarter you in 15 minutes."
- http://www.blinkist.com

Blinkist is a free service (with a paid alternative) that has *"1,000+ best-selling nonfiction books, transformed into powerful packs you can read in just 15 minutes".*

How awesome is that!?

Ok, this may seem like cheating to some of you, but it isn't. I've done the exercise of reading a full book, and then reading the "blink" version of it, and they do a pretty good job at summarizing the main ideas. And as I said before, some books have excessive padding, and their main ideas could perfectly be fitted into less than 3750 words (my calculation of 15 minutes at 250 wpm).

You can use this to get a better understanding of what a book is about before reading it, or you can use it to avoid reading the book. Either way, this is a great way of maximizing your time for acquiring new knowledge. But of course not all can be blinked, a book like this one would be a very incomplete "blink" because it is already a condensed version of all its contents. In my opinion, most authors capitalize over smaller-sized ideas to avoid overloading the readers and to give themselves some room for future publications.

Finally, this great service also has some audio versions of their blinks, and these are a magnificent way to learn new things as we do some mindless tasks, like washing, walking, commuting, etc. This is what I use to help myself stay updated with new and upcoming titles in topics of my interest. And speaking of audio, we will go through Audiobooks in the next section.

Interesting note: If you add up how many words are used in all the "In a Blink" sections of this book, your answer would be approx. 4200 words.

Audiobooks

"I'm kind of old-school and love nothing more than sitting, opening a book, and reading it. But I also love listening to audio books."
- Nick Cave

Audiobooks are yet another form of acquiring knowledge. This medium is a good way to "read" books when you don't actually feel like reading. It is also a good way to help you improve second language skills, as you can listen to proper pronunciation while following written text. Audiobooks have the added advantage of having the possibility of using increased speed to go through them, which would be equivalent to speed reading.

What you need to be careful with regarding audio books, and podcast, and videos for that matter, is to choose very wisely when to multitask; we have already established that multitasking is bad for your cognitive capacity, it damps your productivity, and it might render your time futile. If you choose to listen to podcasts, videos or audiobooks while working out, please only do so for cardio workouts (bicycle, elliptical, treadmills, etc.). For machines and body weight, it is important to be focused on your technique to avoid injuries. Try to consume this kind of media on a time slot dedicated to it, or while partaking in mindless tasks. These tasks would be habits that you do in auto mode like washing dishes, hanging and folding clothes, commuting, etc. For other activities that require your full attention, like driving, or having sex, avoid listening to content. Unless that's what floats your boat.

When choosing what to "listen to", you might find some guidance if you go through recommended literature. This is considered curated content and it is the topic of the following section.

Curated Content

"Select, organize, and present (online content, merchandise, information, etc.), typically using professional or expert knowledge."
- Oxford Dictionaries definition of the verb 'curate'

To choose the articles & books I will read, I follow a few curated sources. Since I resonate with the sources' taste in content, I trust that the majority of their selections will please me. I do this instead of following mass media production outlets, which will publish content to satisfy all tastes and aim for higher exposure. I'll list some of the ones I follow, and some others that my brother (whom in my opinion is the most avid of all learners) recommended, but haven't got around to using them as I'm limiting my information-consumption habits:

- **Tim Ferriss' newsletter and five-bullet Fridays:** Life Hacking and productivity.
- **Pocket's Recommendations:** All topics.
- **Farnam Street's weekly newsletter**: Learning, thinking and Non-fiction Books.
- **Harper's Weekly:** t's a funny, quirky, short, sweet and informative summary of world news.
- **3quarksdaily:** A blog about politics, art and science.
- **Page19:** Recommended Books/Blinks to read.

There are also video and podcast curators, but I don't follow any.

That's almost everything you'll see here on information on input (with the exception of the online courses section), we'll switch focus to discuss information output/creation.

Touch Typing

"After a while, I thought it didn't make any sense to use a pick. It's kind of like typing with one finger on each hand instead of using all your fingers."
- Kevin Eubanks

Even if you're not a writer, most of us need to type in our everyday lives. The average typing speed is 40 words per minute. If you increase your typing speed to 60 wpm you'll potentially increase your writing productivity by 50%. But speed is not all there's to it, how you do it matters as well.

Past generations learned how to touch type in school when teaching typewriter mechanography was part of the curriculum. Touch typing is typing on a keyboard without having to look down to accurately and quickly write. Ironically, nowadays everybody uses a keyboard, but typing classes are no longer part of any curriculum.

The problem with finger typing (not using all ten fingers to type, plus having to look at the keyboard) is not only time-inefficient, it's also bad for our body and concentration. The physical side effects of having to look down are stooping and stressing our backs. And having to concentrate on our fingers makes us partially lose focus. Touch typing may seem daunting, but like everything else, we can learn it. Josh Kaufman used touch typing as one of the skills he presented in his book: The first 20 hours, where he says he achieves a high learning curve during the first 20 hours of deliberate practice. If you want an elaborate way of learning how to touch type, you can try his methodology (check out his book's reference in the Bibliography & Additional References). For me, I prefer something easier to stick to, that's why I use another resource instead: Keybr.com

Keybr is a free resource that capitalizes on muscle memory

and incremental overload. It also has some pretty good analytics to track your progress. When you have enough time and conviction to learn how to touch type, set aside 45 minutes daily to practice in Keybr.com until you reach your desired typing speed. I would also recommend listening to music while doing so, as this will help you master the mechanical motions faster. As in other cases, this is one option among many that you may find on Google.

Sometimes typing faster is not the fastest way to compose a full & finished text. In an unbelievably amount of cases, you can use some automation to get the typing part done for you, you'll learn how in the next section.

Automation

> *"The first rule of any technology used in a business is that automation applied to an efficient operation will magnify the efficiency. The second is that automation applied to an inefficient operation will magnify the inefficiency."*
> - Bill Gates

We have already discussed automation and how automating helps you boost your productivity. In our day and age, apps and software are the most accessible means of automation. We get tailored programs to help us perform things in our day to day lives. But this is not the only way we can automate our digital devices. You might be familiar with automation tools likes Macros in Excel. These allow you to perform time-consuming tasks by just clicking one button, or with a combination of keys (hotkeys). Imagine being able to program your computer to do any combination of clicks, commands, etc. at your will: this is full automation.

We could summarize the elements of automation in the following:

1. Text Expanders:

Text expanders allow you to declare a short string of text that will become an expanded text. For example: when I type "tbr" on my computer I get "Thank you and Best regards," automatically, which is pretty neat. Expanding text like this will save you a lot of typing. You can use it for:

- **Common expressions:** opening phrases, closing phrases, signatures, websites, etc.
- **Canned responses:** If you analyze the kind of emails you send, you'll probably find patterns that you could accommodate in "templates," that you

can just modify slightly (a name here, a word there). These are canned responses, and they will make your life much easier.

- I   use   FastKeys   for   this: http://www.fastkeys.vze.com

2. Macros/Executables:

These are sets of clicks, selections, text strings and commands that you can create to perform tasks automatically. An example would be activating a macro that will open all the programs you normally use, great for triggering after starting your computer.

- I also use FastKeys for this.

3. Gestures:

These are patterns you do with your mouse or trackpad, and that will run a macro or an executable. The gestures are normally triggered by a combination of a mouse click (like clicking the middle scrolling button) and drawing a figure with the cursor. The gesture could also be initiated by a designated pressed key. You can do things like minimizing all windows (a.k.a boss key) or open a new word document (by drawing a W gesture with your mouse).

- I use FastKeys for this too. I know! FastKeys is damn good.

4. **Text Replacement:**

Imagine you need to modify more than one text with some tricky replacement rules, like changing groups of words, differentiating between lower and upper cases, changing complete paragraphs, only modifying indented lines, etc. Sure, you can use Find and Replace functions, but you have to perform each action one by one, and document by document.

The alternative is to define all the rules of text replacement, and then just going document by document and changing them with one single click. I use this automation mostly for programming: I use code generators, which usually have bulky and unnecessary code, which is highly inefficient to delete and modify manually everytime I update the code; in these cases Text Replacement automation saves me hours of work!

- I use TextMage for this: http://www.textmage.com/

5. **Smartphone:**

Just like the other types above, you can set rules in your smartphone to execute certain actions. In smartphones it's pretty cool, you can use the input from the device sensors to trigger the tasks. So you can set it to change automatically the volume or connectivity, say, depending on location, time, battery level, etc. This automation allows you to customize your phone in ways that would otherwise require many apps. I would suggest this for geeks only (I consider myself a geek by the way), is not very straight forward.

- I use Tasker (Android) for this: http://deft.xyz/1RCWC78

6. Web Services and Portals:

There are many web services that help us perform our daily tasks better, or to interact with each other, or to manage content, and then there are ways of connecting most of the services we use and creating rules to use input from one web service to take action in a different one. An example could be updating your Twitter profile photo if you update your Facebook profile photo. This automation will grab the photo and post it in Twitter without any further action required from you, other than just updating your Facebook photo. But this is useful in many more ways than just social media, you can also integrate services at the business level.

The two leaders are Zapier and IFTTT (If this then that). I use IFTTT (https://ifttt.com/). There are other alternatives (free and paid) for these automation, you'll find more resources below. These services can also be used for scheduling posts, using posts from one social media to re-post in other automatically, to collect data using actions (and store it into a google sheet for example) and many other cool things (even replace, to some extent, the Smartphone automation) . Check out their recipes to get more ideas!

I would love to go on automation and tell you how I clean my floors with a little army of cleaning robots, but that stuff isn't really productive at work, unless you're in the cleaning business, so we'll wrap it up here. And now, as promised before, we'll go back to information input one last time. We'll go through online courses to expand your skills in our last section of this chapter!

Udemy, Coursera, and Others

"Live as if you were to die tomorrow. Learn as if you were to live forever."
- Mahatma Gandhi

Learning new things keeps your mind alive, and allows you to create new mental networks that ultimately let you improve your creativity and your understanding of the world and its inhabitants. Learning adds things to your life, so you can always work towards development in areas that you are passionate about it.

For most of our history, we have had very limited resources to learn new things. Now you can virtually learn anything, and even for free. But free isn't always the best way, or at least not the most effective. To ensure high-quality learning material, we now have resources like Udemy, Coursera, EdX, Khan Academy, Udacity, Teachable, and the list goes on. All of these platforms have their pros and cons. But they are all valuable ways to acquire new knowledge and develop skills.

In the matter of productivity, I strongly suggest heading to Coursera and exploring their specializations. The certificates allow you to showcase your acquired knowledge, choose which ones will help grow your career and invest in yourself. EdX also has this possibility. For less academy-oriented courses, Udemy has a pretty good catalog, plus if you're not satisfied, you can get your money back guaranteed (over a 30 days period, no questions asked).

In my case, I used Coursera to re-create an MBA-like curriculum to improve my management skills to perform better at my previous position as Service Delivery Manager for Gabon and West Africa, if this interests you, please check out: http://blog.deft.xyz/learning-projects/. Prior to that, I took a dozen of courses in Udemy to learn how to speed and power read, learn to meditate, get some basic on project management, practice French, and some other random topics.

Congratulations! You've reached the end of the Information Management chapter. In this one, you learned some techniques to process audio and video more quickly, how to power and speed read, cool ways of choosing content to consume, and ways to optimize your information creation.

In a Blink

Let's review the main ideas of this chapter in a blink.

Speed Controls: Video & Audio

Two of the most efficient ways to consume information are videos and audio. To help you go through new information faster, you can use speed control options to view/listen content at 1.5X or even 2X (whatever speed you feel comfortable with).

An alternative to browser base speed controls, you can use the software MySpeed, which also allows you some offline functionality.

Power -and Speed- Reading

Since the way you learned how to read in elementary school didn't get any updates along the years, the following techniques will serve as a major update and probably increase your reading speed (from the average 250 words per minute) up to 200% or 300% times faster, while improving retention and engagement. Now, the main principles of power reading:

1. **Choose what to read.**
2. **Establish how will you read it.**
3. **Expand your visual horizon.**
4. **Reduce subvocalization.**
5. **Avoid regressing.**
6. **Pause to recall.**
7. **Choose what to re-read and what to skip.**

Blinkist

Blinkist is a free service (with a paid alternative) that has "1,000+ best-selling nonfiction books, transformed into powerful packs you can read in just 15 minutes". Very useful to stay updated in new books coming out, and to explore before committing to full-length books.

Audiobooks

Audiobooks are yet another form of acquiring knowledge. A particularly easy one to follow and that has the added benefit of allowing you to speed it up, which effectively makes it equal to speed reading.

Curated Content

Instead of aimlessly consuming media, you can choose the articles & books to read from curated sources. You can look for sources that resonate with you, to make it easier to choose content. In my case, these sources are Tim Ferriss' newsletter and five-bullet Fridays, Pocket's Recommendations, Farnam Street's weekly newsletter, Harper's weekly review, 3quarksdaily, and Page19.

Touch Typing

Even if you're not a writer, you're likely to need to type in your everyday life (emails, reports, SMS, tinder, and whatnot). The average typing speed is 40 wpm, by increasing it to 60 wpm you'll potentially increase your writing productivity by 50%. But touch typing is not only about typing, it is also about using all ten fingers to type, while not looking at your keyboard. This will also add benefits ergonomically and in favor of focus. I recommend using Keybr for 45 minutes daily while listening to music, until you reach your desired typing speed.

Automation

Automation helps you boost your productivity. In digital terms, we could summarize the elements of automation in the following:

1. **Text Expanders:** Convert short strings into longer text (like common expressions) or canned responses.
2. **Macros/Executables:** These are sets of clicks, selections, text strings and commands to perform tasks automatically.
3. **Gestures:** You can trigger events by drawing patterns with your mouse or trackpad, which in turn can execute macros or specific commands (like executing a program). For this, and the previous two I use FastKeys.
4. **Text Replacement:** This automation consists of complex text modifications done in any text length in one run, instead of having to perform multiple manual searches and replaces. I use TextMage for this.
5. **Smartphone:** You can use your smartphone's features to execute commands and automate functions. This is not very straight forward. I use Tasker (Android) for this.
6. **Web Services and Portals:** You can use services like Zapier and IFTTT to connect several web services and run recipes to make your digital life easier.

Udemy, Coursera, and Others

Today you can find endless learning resources to help you expand your skills and job-specific knowledge. I recommend Coursera and Edx for career-based learning, including specializations. And I recommend Udemy for other non-academic learning topics, like music, languages, speed reading, etc.

Chapter 8: Wrap-Up

Thank You!

You've reached the end of the book! I knew you were amazing from the moment you decided to buy my book! Ok, ok, just kidding! But I did trust that you had all the intentions and drive to get to this point.

The main objective of the book is to help you get more out of life by helping increase your productivity. Try to put these speedster's abilities to good use, by working every day to make your life a happier and more memorable one, and by doing so, making the life of those around you a better one as well.

Although you might not want to implement EVERYTHING you've learned throughout the book, even the smallest one you do adhere to will help you immensely to keep believing in self-improvement. I would still urge you to try to use as many of these tools as possible, but little by little so you don't crash and burn in the attempt. Be kind to yourself and remember that a few slips and mistakes will make you stronger.

I hope you found this book interesting, inspiring, and ultimately useful to you. It was a great process for me, and I'm a more fulfilled person by having written it. So, if you did like it, spread the love and recommend the book to your friends and co-workers!

Before you close the book, I would like to invite you to subscribe to my blog: http://blog.deft.xyz/ where I post articles about productivity, learning, leadership, and other interesting topics.

Thank you and Best regards, (yes, I wrote that using the "tbr" text expansion)

David F. Suescun R.

PS: Feel free to write to me directly, although I'm not sure if I'll be able to respond to all inquiries, but I'll sure try my best to do so! My email is dashja@gmail.com
PPS: Also, feel free to follow me:
Facebook: https://www.facebook.com/dsuescun/
Twitter: https://twitter.com/DavidSuescunR/
and   LinkedIn:
https://www.linkedin.com/in/davidsuescun/

PPPS: Don't forget to join our Facebook Community Page at http://deft.xyz/1pi7DlX

About the Author

David Suescun
Mechatronics Engineer, Life Hacker, Entrepreneur and Learning Junkie.

David Suescun dreams with a world where people don't have to overstay at work, can manage their time to enjoy their family and friends and live fulfilling lives.

As a Mechatronics Engineer, Oil & Gas Professional, Author, Musician, Developer and Entrepreneur, he has created digital products (Software for Texas Instruments calculators, Windows Software and Android & iOS Apps) with over 200 thousand joint downloads, recorded over 80 songs, written a book on productivity and founded an App development company. Has an eight years' experience in Oil & Gas working in field operations, management, marketing and quality assurance in five countries. As a self-learning junkie, he has successfully completed more than 50 online courses on a wide range of topics, including completing an MBA equivalent curriculum he designed by himself. Learned English, Portuguese and French while living in his country, Colombia.

When he's not devouring new knowledge on Lifehacking, Productivity, and Leadership, you can find him developing new projects and hanging out with his family and friends, fixing the world of course.

This book got him to branch out and create an Udemy course and support it with an ever growing Community Page and a Productivity & Learning Blog (http://deft.xyz).

Bibliography & Additional References

For the sake of simplicity, the bibliography has been added only in the chapter of its first reference. Also, I've provided the links for the readers' convenience, but they might change or be discontinued by the original publishers, if you encounter a broken link, please let me know and I'll correct it in the next revised edition.

Chapter 1:
- N/A

Chapter 2:
1. Pappas, Christopher. "The Adult Learning Theory - Andragogy - of Malcolm Knowles." Blog. eLearning Industry, May 9, 2013. *http://deft.xyz/1ifPIbY*
2. Keller, Gary, and Jay Papasan. *The ONE Thing: The Surprisingly Simple Truth Behind Extraordinary Results*. 1 edition. Austin, Texas: Bard Press, 2013. *http://amzn.to/1nhCz4R*
3. TEDx Talks. *Learning How to Learn | Barbara Oakley | TEDx Oakland University*. Accessed October 25, 2015. *http://deft.xyz/1S8CUAX*
4. Oakley, Barbara. *A Mind for Numbers: How to Excel at Math and Science*. New York: Tarcher, 2014. *http://deft.xyz/1H9s7QD*
5. Kashdan, Todd, and Robert Biswas-Diener. The Upside of Your Dark Side: Why Being Your Whole Self--Not Just Your "Good" Self--Drives Success and Fulfillment. Reprint edition. Plume, 2015. *http://amzn.to/1lHYJfr*

6. Ferriss, Timothy. *The 4-Hour Workweek: Escape 9-5, Live Anywhere, and Join the New Rich*. Exp Upd edition. New York: Harmony, 2009. *http://amzn.to/1ZLlOvd*

7. Koch, Richard. *The 80/20 Principle: The Secret to Achieving More with Less*. Reprint edition. New York: Crown Business, 1999. *http://amzn.to/1lHZ4yW*

8. "Parkinson's Law." *Wikipedia, the Free Encyclopedia*, October 21, 2015. *http://deft.xyz/1Wm2aJW*

9. Ariga, Atsunori, and Alejandro Lleras. "Brief and Rare Mental 'breaks' Keep You Focused: Deactivation and Reactivation of Task Goals Preempt Vigilance Decrements." Cognition 118, no. 3 (March 2011): 439–43. doi:10.1016/j.cognition.2010.12.007. *http://deft.xyz/1OX9S90*

10. Gifford, Julia. "The Rule of 52 and 17: It's Random, But It Ups Your Productivity." The Muse. Accessed October 24, 2015. *http://deft.xyz/1SETQ5g*

11. Stillman, Jessica. "How to Learn to Be Luckier." *Inc.com*, August 14, 2014. *http://deft.xyz/1PTpZ6L*

12. Wiseman, Richard. "Be Lucky - It's an Easy Skill to Learn," January 9, 2003, sec. Technology. *http://deft.xyz/1O6xQhU*

13. Wiseman, Richard. Luck Factor. New Ed edition. London: Arrow Books Ltd, 2004. *http://amzn.to/1nhDB0E*

14. Chansky, Tamar. "8 Strategies For Making A Better Life." *The Huffington Post*, February 6, 2012. *http://deft.xyz/1H9tyOY*

15. "How To Overcome Perfectionism." AnxietyBC. Accessed October 24, 2015. *http://deft.xyz/1LXGERt*

16. Csikszentmihalyi, Mihaly. *Flow, the Secret to Happiness*, Filmed Feb, 2004. *http://deft.xyz/1N6HVKn*

17. Fabrega, Marelisa. "How To Enter the Flow State." *Daring to Live Fully*. Accessed October 1, 2015. *http://deft.xyz/1PTqKNd*

18. "Willpower." *Merriam-Webster Dictionary*. Accessed October 30, 2015. *http://deft.xyz/1My1gFz*

19. Coleman, John. "Faced with Distraction, We Need Willpower." *Harvard Business Review*, February 22, 2012. *http://deft.xyz/1N6IgwC*

20. Baumeister, Roy F., and John Tierney. Willpower: Rediscovering the Greatest Human Strength. Reprint edition. New York: Penguin Books, 2012. *http://amzn.to/1nhE2rR*

21. McGonigal, Kelly. The Willpower Instinct: How Self-Control Works, Why It Matters, and What You Can Do to Get More of It. Reprint edition. Avery, 2013. *http://amzn.to/1ZLng0O*

22. Duhigg, Charles. The Power of Habit: Why We Do What We Do in Life and Business. New York: Random House Trade Paperbacks, 2014. *http://amzn.to/1PeuAAq*

23. Schmeichel, Brandon J., Kathleen D. Vohs, and Roy F. Baumeister. "Intellectual Performance and Ego Depletion: Role of the Self in Logical Reasoning and Other Information Processing." Journal of Personality and Social Psychology 85, no. 1 (2003): 33–46. doi:10.1037/0022-3514.85.1.33. *http://deft.xyz/1NzOVOi*

24. "Ego Depletion." *Wikipedia, the Free Encyclopedia*, September 16, 2015. *http://deft.xyz/1ijUwxO*

25. Barnes, Christopher M., Brian Gunia, and Sunita Sah. "Morning People Are Less Ethical at Night." *Harvard Business Review*, June 23, 2014. *http://deft.xyz/1NzP0Bx*

26. Ferriss, Timothy. "Understanding the Dangers of 'Ego-Depletion.'" *The Blog of Author Tim Ferriss*, August 12, 2012. *http://deft.xyz/209kfKG*

27. Smith, Jacquelyn. "Steve Jobs Always Dressed Exactly the Same. Here's Who Else Does." *Forbes*, October 5, 2012. *http://deft.xyz/1S8Ewe6*

28. Ravenscraft, Eric. "Use Louis CK's 70% Rule to Avoid Decision Paralysis." *Lifehacker*, May 1, 2014. *http://deft.xyz/209krtj*

Chapter 3:

29. Duhigg, Charles. The Power of Habit: Why We Do What We Do in Life and Business. New York: Random House Trade Paperbacks, 2014. *http://deft.xyz/1WhQMcR*

30. Lally, Phillippa, Cornelia H. M. van Jaarsveld, Henry W. W. Potts, and Jane Wardle. "How Are Habits Formed: Modelling Habit Formation in the Real World." European Journal of Social Psychology 40, no. 6 (October 1, 2010): 998–1009. doi:10.1002/ejsp.674. *http://deft.xyz/1H9vfvP*

31. Oakley, Barbara. A Mind for Numbers: How to Excel at Math and Science. New York: Tarcher, 2014. *http://deft.xyz/1H9s7QD*

32. Learning How to Learn | Barbara Oakley | TEDx Oakland University. Accessed October 25, 2015. *http://deft.xyz/1S8CUAX*

33. Strongly recommend taking this free MOOC course: http://deft.xyz/1WgYObc

34. "Testing Effect." Wikipedia, the Free Encyclopedia, August 19, 2015. *http://deft.xyz/1H9vIh*

35. Scott H. Young's Blog *http://www.scotthyoung.com/*

36. Memrise's Website *https://www.memrise.com/*

37. Anki's Website *http://ankisrs.net/*

Chapter 4:

38. Follow-up and Task Planner Excel file: *http://deft.xyz/1UfTnpO*

39. Ferriss, Timothy. "The Not-To-Do List: 9 Habits to Stop Now." The Blog of Author Tim Ferriss, August 16, 2007. *http://deft.xyz/1k8wHJy*

40. Wang, Zheng. "MULTITASKING MAY HURT YOUR PERFORMANCE, BUT IT MAKES YOU FEEL BETTER." The Ohio State University Research and Innovation Communications, April 30, 2012. *http://deft.xyz/1LXJjuE*

41. Gorlick, Adam. "Media Multitaskers Pay Mental Price, Stanford Study Shows." Stanford University, August 24, 2009. *http://deft.xyz/1NzPzeJ*

42. "Multitasking: Switching Costs." American Psychological Association, March 20, 2006. *http://deft.xyz/1LBarlc*

43. Fitzpatrick, Jason. "A Case for Singletasking: The One-Task-At-a-Time Method." Lifehacker, September 24, 2010. *http://deft.xyz/1kPAAUB*

44. Pattison, Kermit. "Worker, Interrupted: The Cost of Task Switching." Fast Company, July 28, 2008. *http://deft.xyz/1M1gTDo*

45. Covey, Stephen R., A. Roger Merrill, and Rebecca R. Merrill. First Things First. Reprint edition. New York: Free Press, 1996. *http://deft.xyz/1LXJPsq*

46. "MoSCoW Method." Wikipedia, the Free Encyclopedia, October 20, 2015. *http://deft.xyz/1XxTuxk*

47. "10. MoSCoW Prioritisation." Driving Strategy Delivering More. Accessed October 25, 2015. *http://deft.xyz/1Ms5VsL*

48. RescueTime's website: *https://www.rescuetime.com*

49. StayFocusd's Chrome Extension page: *http://deft.xyz/1Mlk7xp*

Chapter 5:

50. Schwartz, Tony, and Catherine McCarthy. "Manage Your Energy, Not Your Time." Harvard Business Review, October 1, 2007. *http://deft.xyz/1OaUrdp*

51. Covey, Stephen R. The 7 Habits of Highly Effective People: Powerful Lessons in Personal Change. Anniversary Edition edition. New York: Simon & Schuster, 2013. *http://deft.xyz/1XCGaI6*

52. Stenudd, Stefan. "Qi Breathing Exercises, Use Your Breath to Stimulate Your Qi Flow." Qi Energy Exercises. Accessed October 25, 2015. *http://deft.xyz/1Scgyic*

53. Weil, Andrew. "Three Breathing Exercises and Techniques." WEIL. Accessed October 26, 2015. *http://deft.xyz/1NbuMzU*

54. USDA's 2015-2020 Dietary Guidelines for Americans *http://deft.xyz/1P6Fhl3*

55. My app for increasing strength: 6 Weeks 2 Fit *http://onelink.to/6w2fit*

56. Warner, Jennifer. "Exercise Fights Fatigue, Boosts Energy." WebMD, November 3, 2006. *http://deft.xyz/1k8pSb7*

57. Crilly, Meredith. "What Happens to Mitochondria During Aerobic Exercise?" Live Healthy - Chron.com. Accessed October 26, 2015. *http://deft.xyz/1XxQUqW*

58. Smith, Jessica. "Energy Usage During Exercise: How It Affects Your Workouts." Accessed October 25, 2015. *http://deft.xyz/1KEngHu*

59. Burgomaster, Kirsten A., Krista R. Howarth, Stuart M. Phillips, Mark Rakobowchuk, Maureen J. MacDonald, Sean L. McGee, and Martin J. Gibala. "Similar Metabolic Adaptations during Exercise after Low Volume Sprint Interval and Traditional Endurance Training in Humans." The Journal of Physiology 586, no. 1 (January 1, 2008): 151–60. doi:10.1113/jphysiol.2007.142109. *http://deft.xyz/1Ms0zxC*

60. Fung, Jason. "Exercise Is Not Total Energy Expenditure." Intensive Dietary Management, May 8, 2015. *http://deft.xyz/1RAtKfU*

61. Menshikova, Elizabeth V., Vladimir B. Ritov, Liane Fairfull, Robert E. Ferrell, David E. Kelley, and Bret H. Goodpaster. "Effects of Exercise on Mitochondrial Content and Function in Aging Human Skeletal Muscle." The Journals of Gerontology. Series A, Biological Sciences and Medical Sciences 61, no. 6 (June 2006): 534–40. *http://deft.xyz/1MSwXUs*

62. Freeletics' website *https://www.freeletics.com/r/1755841*

63. "How Much Can an Extra Hour's Sleep Change You?" BBC News, October 9, 2013. *http://deft.xyz/209gzsi*

64. Mann, Denise. "Can Better Sleep Mean Catching Fewer Colds?" WebMD, January 19, 2010. *http://deft.xyz/1MrZaad*

65. Wiseman, Richard. Night School: Wake up to the Power of Sleep. Place of publication not identified: CreateSpace Independent Publishing Platform, 2014. *http://amzn.to/24JVVkV*

66. Reddy, Sumathi. "Find the Perfect Sleep Position." Wall Street Journal, January 14, 2013, sec. Health and Wellness. *http://deft.xyz/1GwtIW5*

67. Giang, Vivian. "Our Poor Sleeping Habits Are Filling Our Brains with Neurotoxins." Quartz, June 10, 2015. *http://deft.xyz/1WhPpe2*

68. Kolowich, Lindsay. "The Science of Sleep: What Happens During the 5 Stages of Your Sleep Cycle [Infographic]." HubSpot Blogs, August 5, 2015. *http://deft.xyz/209htVQ*

69. Park, Alice. "How Booze Messes With Your Sleep." Time, January 16, 2015. *http://deft.xyz/1MhvI0v*

70. Emotional Intelligence 2.0 Note: Get it from their website so you can get a digital version + test access *http://www.talentsmart.com/products/emotional-intelligence-2.0/*

71. Covey, Stephen R. The 8th Habit: From Effectiveness to Greatness. Reprint edition. New York: Free Press, 2005. *http://deft.xyz/1PXkR1z*

72. Bregman, Peter. "If You're Too Busy to Meditate, Read This." Harvard Business Review, October 12, 2012. *http://deft.xyz/1ScgH52*

73. Brady, Adam. "Mindful Walking Practice: How to Get Started." Chopra.com. Accessed November 10, 2015. *http://deft.xyz/1Y2rz93*

74. Kondo, Marie. The Life-Changing Magic of Tidying Up: The Japanese Art of Decluttering and Organizing.

First American Ed First Printing edition. Berkeley: Ten Speed Press, 2014. *http://deft.xyz/1Nbvm0s*

75. Parrish, Shane. "The Japanese Art of Decluttering and Organizing." Farnam Street, December 9, 2014. *http://deft.xyz/1WktisG*

76. I strongly suggest taking this course as it will open your mind to a new and interesting way of seeing the world: *https://www.coursera.org/learn/model-thinking*

77. Parrish, Shane. "An Introduction to Mental Models." Farnam Street. Accessed October 26, 2015. *http://deft.xyz/1NDILN8*

78. Ariely, Dan. Predictably Irrational, Revised and Expanded Edition: The Hidden Forces That Shape Our Decisions. 1 Exp Rev edition. New York: Harper Perennial, 2010. *http://deft.xyz/1M3QYLo*

79. Kahneman, Daniel. Thinking, Fast and Slow. Reprint edition. New York: Farrar, Straus and Giroux, 2013. *http://deft.xyz/1keXTGG*

Chapter 6:

80. "State of the American Workplace." Gallup.com. Accessed October 26, 2015. *http://deft.xyz/1PPZ3FY*

81. Dennett, Daniel C. Intuition Pumps And Other Tools for Thinking. First Edition edition. New York: W. W. Norton & Company, 2013. *http://amzn.to/1nylcwN*

82. Langer, Ellen J., Arthur Blank, and Benzion Chanowitz. "The Mindlessness of Ostensibly Thoughtful Action: The Role of 'Placebic' Information in Interpersonal Interaction." Journal of Personality and Social Psychology 36, no. 6 (1978): 635–42. doi:10.1037/0022-3514.36.6.635. *http://deft.xyz/1k8DxPo*

83. Aral, Sinan, Erik Brynjolfsson, Van Alstyne, and Marshall W. "Harnessing the Digital Lens to Measure and Manage Information Work." SSRN Scholarly Paper. Rochester, NY: Social Science Research

Network, November 16, 2010.
http://deft.xyz/1LBdbyR

84. Pink, Daniel H. Drive: The Surprising Truth About What Motivates Us. New York, NY: Riverhead Books, 2011. *http://deft.xyz/1H9Cl3y*

85. Neville Medhora's copyright blog and course: http://kopywritingkourse.com/

86. "AIDA (marketing)." Wikipedia, the Free Encyclopedia, September 18, 2015. *http://deft.xyz/1kPG9lT*

87. "Copywriting." Wikipedia, the Free Encyclopedia, October 10, 2015. *http://deft.xyz/1PPZ9NV*

88. Folkman, Joseph, and Jack Zenger. "The Ideal Praise-to-Criticism Ratio." Harvard Business Review, March 15, 2013. *http://deft.xyz/1MsaYJv*

Chapter 7:

89. MySpeed's Website: *http://www.enounce.com/*

90. Parrish, Shane. "How to Read A Book." Farnam Street. Accessed October 26, 2015. *http://deft.xyz/1GNptVW*

91. "Eye Movement in Reading." Wikipedia, the Free Encyclopedia, September 4, 2015. *http://deft.xyz/1M3Rg4X*

92. "Speed Reading: Learning to Read More Efficiently." MindTools. Accessed October 26, 2015. *http://deft.xyz/1jVkSqG*

93. Tim Ferriss. How to Triple Your Reading Speed in 20 Minutes (Tim Ferriss), 2015. *http://deft.xyz/1RgUxhs*

94. Blinkist's website: http://jump.blinkist.com/SHPU

95. Widder, Brandon. "16 Great Websites for Free Audiobooks." Digital Trends, April 6, 2015. *http://deft.xyz/1RCWsfY*

96. "Curate." Oxford Dictionaries, n.d. *http://deft.xyz/1MwRrry*

97. To join Farnam Street's newsletter, please go to *https://www.farnamstreetblog.com/newsletter/*

98. To read Pocket's Recommendations, please go to *https://getpocket.com/a/recommended/*
99. To read Tim Ferriss' blog, please go to *http://fourhourworkweek.com/*
100. To read and subscribe to Harper's Weekly, please go to *http://harpers.org/blog/weekly-review/*
101. To read 3quarksdaily's Blog, please go to *http://www.3quarksdaily.com/*
102. To read and subscribe to Page19, please go to *https://www.blinkist.com/page19/*
103. Keybr's Website: *http://www.keybr.com/*
104. Kaufman, Josh. "Chapter 6: Touch Typing." THE FIRST 20 HOURS. Accessed October 25, 2015. *http://deft.xyz/1HeTKYz*
105. FastKeys' Website: *http://www.fastkeys.vze.com*
106. TextMage's Website: *http://www.textmage.com/*
107. Tasker's Google Play URL: *http://deft.xyz/1RCWC78*
108. IFTTT's website: *https://ifttt.com/*
109. Lifehacker's Text Expansion resource page: *http://deft.xyz/1PXpR6q*

Chapter 8:

- N/A

THE END
(Who doesn't dream with writing that on their own book?)